Peter

JESUS CHRIST IS LORD

MARSHALL, MORGAN & SCOTT
London

OTHER BOOKS BY THE SAME AUTHOR

The Emergence of Hyper-Calvinism, 1689–1765 (1967)
Puritans, the Millennium and the Future of Israel (1970)
'Life of William Romaine' in Romaine, *Life, Walk and Triumph of Faith* (1970)
God's Statesman: the Life and Work of John Owen, 1616–1683 (1972)
Puritans and Calvinism (1973)
The Ordinal and its Revision (1974)
Knowing God through the Liturgy (1974)
John Charles Ryle, Evangelical Bishop (1976)
Evangelical Theology, 1833–1856; A Response to Tractarianism (1978)

CONTENTS

Preface	v
1. Introducing the theme	1
2. The exalted Jesus	6
3. Jesus, Messiah and Lord	19
4. The meaning of the Ascension	36
5. Jesus, Lord of the nations	48
6. Jesus, Lord of the Church	64
7. Jesus, Lord of the universe	85
8. Jesus, Lord of all religions	101
9. The exalted Jesus and the Creeds	121
10. Jesus, my Lord	133
Appendix: The Reformers and the Ascension	149

All biblical quotations, unless otherwise stated, are from the Good News Bible, Old Testament © American Bible Society, New York 1976, New Testament © American Bible Society, New York 1966, 1971 and fourth edition 1976 and used by permission of the British and Foreign Bible Society and William Collins Sons & Co. Ltd.

MARSHALL, MORGAN AND SCOTT, a member of the Pentos group, 1 Bath Street, London EC1V 9LB. Copyright © Peter Toon, 1978. First published 1978. ISBN 0 551 05570 7. All rights reserved. No part of this publication may be reproduced, stored in a retrieval system, or transmitted, in any form or by any means, electronic, mechanical, photocopying, recording or otherwise, without the prior permission of the Copyright owner. Printed in Great Britain by J. W. Arrowsmith Ltd., Bristol. 8710L570.

PREFACE

AS YOU ENTER the chapel of Oak Hill Theological College, Southgate, London, there directly in front of you is a magnificent tapestry covering the wall behind the communion table. The design is intended to depict the confession of faith made at baptism, and thus the words 'Jesus Christ is Lord' (2 Cor. 4:5) are at the centre. The constant reading of these words as I worshipped in the chapel provided not only the inspiration to write this book but, at an earlier point in time, the contents of my first sermon in the chapel preached on the occasion of a baptism.

The material presented here is not meant to be new. To serious students of Scripture and theology it is well known. Rather it is a popular presentation of the great theme of the exaltation of Jesus as Lord of all. There are many popular books which expound the Lordship of Christ over the individual life but in this book I have tried to portray Jesus, the Christ, as the universal Lord, Head of the cosmos, the Church and of every human being. For my quotations from Scripture I have used most of the time the Good News Bible.

Most of the material was given in a series of addresses in the College chapel on Monday mornings in Lent 1977. For helpful comments and criticism I am indebted to staff and students, especially to the Rev Josephus Jeyaraj, a presbyter of the Church of South India, Geoffrey Maughan, the senior student, and Richard Ginn.

I would like to dedicate this book to Kristina, who will be baptised this year, and to her parents Jeffrey and Debbie Steenson.

Lent 1977

Peter Toon
Oak Hill College
London N14

1 Introducing the theme

THE EARLIEST CHRISTIAN confession of faith was 'Jesus Christ is Lord'. Within the Christian community, and to those who made this declaration, these four words summarised a very high estimate of the carpenter's son Jesus of Nazareth, and included a high view of the meaning of human existence in history, and a conviction about the purpose and future of the universe. Today, in our Western culture, the word 'Lord' does not convey the possibilities of meaning which *kyrios*, the word it translates, did in the Graeco-Roman world in which the New Testament was written. That is, we do not possess a single word which can signify and convey everything which 'Lord' could for the Greek-speaking Christian.

Nevertheless, the Church today and the world in which the Church is set needs, as much as did the world of the first century after Christ, the good news of One who remarkably is both God and Man, who has lived a full human life, died, risen from the dead, and who now rules the universe for the good of mankind and the glory of God, Creator of the universe. Our task in this book is to attempt to explain what the Lordship of Jesus Christ means for Christian faith today.

Knowledge of, and submission to, the Lordship of Jesus Christ has always been a basic constituent of Christianity. Today, it is needed perhaps more than ever before because of the complex and varied nature of the pressures and temptations in which we live within our Western society.... This century has witnessed an erosion of traditional sources and views of authority and inevitably, since the Church is affected by its environment, the authority of Christ in his Church has been diminished. He competes with other 'lords', be they the laws of sociology or psychology, or the pronouncements of the scientist. But, apart from this general erosion, the authority of Jesus Christ for Western man has been devalued by specific factors. Let us notice several of these.

In recent times the story of success by scientists and technologists has been phenomenal. Men have been to the Moon; hearts and livers have been transplanted from one human to another; the radio telescope has opened up to us vast galaxies millions of light years away; our houses now have deep-freezers instead of cold, deep cellars; we clean the house with an electric cleaner, only rarely with a brush, and we watch television programmes coming live from thousands of miles away beamed by a satellite; and when we travel it is not by foot, carriage and steamship but by car, diesel-electric train and either Jumbo or Concorde jet. Because of these and many other 'triumphs' the status of 'science' has been elevated so that many people regard the word of the scientist as the final word and, even more regrettably, the world investigated by the scientist as the only reality. The world of the spirit, the supernatural, the reality we call God, since they cannot be seen, investigated or conquered are denied, forgotten or discounted. For such people Jesus Christ may have value but it is only as a teacher of morals. If he has Lordship it is narrow and shallow in scope.

Another powerful reality in modern life is what is called 'economic factors'. The price of raw materials for industry, of oil for machinery and vehicles, of the value of the pound sterling or the mighty US dollar, all affect the cost of food, clothing and housing for people from all income-brackets, and no individual person can do anything about it. We are all subject, it seems, to forces controlling the nature of our daily lives. We are caught up in an economic spider's web; we are subject to the lordship of the market-forces. Where, it is asked, is the Lordship of Christ in all this? Rich countries are not subject to his Lordship when they sell goods to poorer countries at high rates, and oil-exporting countries are not subject to his Lordship when they keep on raising the cost of oil and thus cause inflation with all its attendant problems.

To a degree which few of us realise we are all also subject, to a lesser or a greater extent, to powerful indoctrination by value-systems which operate through the mass media, glossy magazines, advertisements in shops and on railway platforms, and in contemporary films, plays, novels and poetry. A word widely used to describe the confusion of moral standards or the abandonment of old ones is 'permissiveness'. That is, one is permitted to desire, and then to have, what one cannot afford (a better car) or what belongs to another (sexual relations with the married partner of another). What was once regarded as unsuitable for public viewing and reading is now commonplace—for example, the many occasions in modern films, plays and novels when sexual intercourse is intimately described or acted out. Truthfulness and faithfulness are regarded as old-fashioned to be replaced by vagueness and carelessness. The Lordship of Christ over moral systems and behaviour patterns appears to be a very rare phenomenon in today's world.

And even in the churches where one would expect to hear a clear statement that Jesus is Lord there is often a confused and confusing confession of faith being made. The impact of the study of, and encounter with, other religions—Islam, Hinduism and Buddhism, for example—has apparently weakened the confession that Jesus Christ is the unique Lord. The impact of the behavioural sciences (psychology, sociology, etc.) has weakened confidence in Christian views of sin and salvation in human nature and the impact of other sciences has brought a whole series of questions concerning the origin of the universe and of the species, miracles and life after death. To make matters worse the theologians, to whom Christians look as 'servants of Christ and his Church' appear to lead the way in destroying Christianity instead of defending 'the faith which once and for all God has given to his people' (Jude 3). Jesus Christ appears not to be Lord of his Church in any obvious and visible sense.

What do we say in the face of all this? Apart from the sad situation in some of our churches, we should not be surprised that the Lordship of Christ does not apparently operate in our society. We live in a period of human history in which evil and sin have not been removed from human nature and human institutions. The Lordship is best described, in terms of its relationship to the world, as eschatological. It will only become a universal, observable reality at the end of the age when Christ returns to earth 'in power and great glory' as King of the nations and Judge of all men. Meanwhile, that is between his Ascension and Second Coming, his Lordship over the whole cosmos is appreciated only by the mind of faith and seen only by the eye of faith. Jesus Christ certainly rules, but his rule is secret as far as the material eye and mind are concerned. However, in his Church his rule is meant to be seen: in the community of those who are joined to him by faith and through the Holy Spirit his kingdom of love and grace is meant to be visible. In the worship, fellowship, evangelism, behaviour and business administration of the Church Christ should rule as King. Likewise he is meant to be King in the life of the individual Christian. Furthermore, as we shall see, his Lordship has relevance to the structures of human society.

2 The exalted Jesus

THERE HAVE BEEN many attempts to write the Life of Jesus. Our grandparents had many 'biographies' of Jesus from which to choose, and as we look over our collections of old books in our homes and churches we can still easily find such studies as *The Life and Times of Jesus The Messiah* (1883) by Alfred Edersheim, *The Life of Christ* (1870) by Dean F. W. Farrar and also T. R. Glover's *The Jesus of History* (1917).

Since the Second World War such published lives of Jesus have decreased. One major reason for this has been the general agreement by scholars that the Gospels in the Bible are not intended as biographies but rather as statements, making use of a biographical format, of 'the Good News of Jesus, the Christ'. We know that only two of the four give details of the birth of Jesus and only one mentions incidents between the birth of Jesus and the beginning of his public ministry. Then we are aware that a large proportion of the text of the Gospels is given over to the Passion narrative, that description of the week leading up to the Crucifixion of Jesus in Jerusalem.

Taking these and other matters into account we now generally agree that it is impossible to write a life of Jesus, for the information is missing for nearly thirty years of his life and the majority of the information we have relates to specific parts of his whole earthly life. This said, there is still in the popular, public mind, and probably also in the devout Christian mind, a desire to have a life of Jesus: and in order to satisfy the former we have seen in recent times two popular musicals, *Jesus Christ, Super-*

star and *Godspell*, and to satisfy the latter Professor Dodd's scholarly but eminently readable *The Founder of Christianity* (1971) and Dr Donald Guthrie's *Jesus the Messiah* (1972).

Two parts to the life of Jesus

Christians believe and the churches confess in their creeds that Jesus, the Christ, is the Son of God in a full human nature, that is with a human body and mind. John wrote that 'The Word [*Logos*] was made flesh and dwelt among us' (John 1:14 RSV) and Peter declared that Jesus, the Rabbi, was the Christ, the Son of the living God (Matt. 16:16 RSV). Within the womb of the Virgin Mary the Son of God entered into a union with a humanity derived from Mary and from that moment of conception the Son had a human life as well as a divine life. His divine life is from everlasting to everlasting; it is eternal and infinite since it is the divine life shared by the Father and the Holy Spirit. The Nicene Creed affirms that he is 'one in being with the Father', and 'true God from true God'. In contrast, his human life began at a specific point in space and time, that is in Bethlehem in ancient Palestine, and it will exist (as far as we know from Scripture) everlastingly. This human life of the Son of God may be divided into two unequal parts.

The first runs from his birth of the Virgin Mary until his crucifixion by Roman soldiers on a hill outside Jerusalem. The period covered here is between thirty and thirty-three years and includes the life in Egypt as a baby, as a youth and a man in Nazareth and about three years of public ministry in Galilee and Judea with an occasional trip to districts such as Caesarea Philippi. All our knowledge of this life in terms of biographical information, content of his teaching and the reaction of others to him is found in the four Gospels.

The second part of the human life of the Son of God is a much longer period stretching from the Resurrection and Ascension on the one side to the return in glory at the other. All our knowledge of this life, lived in heaven, is derived from the Acts of the Apostles, the Epistles and the Revelation, together with important insights and hints from John's Gospel. The Apostle Paul told the Corinthians that 'if at one time we judged [viewed] Christ according to human standards, we no longer do so' (2 Cor. 5: 16). In saying this he was not devaluing the historical basis of Christianity for he was the very preacher who insisted much on the death of Christ on the cross—we preach, he claimed, Christ crucified (1 Cor. 1:23). But the Christ he knew as an apostle from the time of his dramatic call on the road to Damascus (Acts 9) was the same Son of God who existed in the fullness of glorified human nature behind and beyond the veil of sense but who nevertheless existed as truly as he had done in Palestine in the days of his life there. Even as men and women had known him as the Rabbi from Nazareth and had followed him as Master, so now in the period after his Ascension, Paul and the early Christians knew him as the One who was shaping their lives and the events through which they lived. By his Spirit Jesus the Christ was known to them.

This heavenly life of Jesus, the exalted Christ, cannot of course be written about or talked about in the same way that it is possible to talk about his actual walking, talking, eating and sleeping in Galilee or Judea. Our human languages have been designed by us in order to describe finite, temporal existence and experience and thus when we, as did the Apostles, come to talk about that which lies beyond the scope of the human eye or radio telescope we must use a kind of non-literal picture language—to be more precise we must speak analogically or symbolically. For example, when we say 'Jesus Christ sits at the right hand of the Father in heaven' we do not intend to be understood as saying that there is a golden throne in heaven like that, for example, used in Westminster Abbey when a British monarch is crowned and on this heavenly throne sits the Father by the side of whom on a less glorious throne sits the exalted Christ. Rather we use a familiar picture in order to convey the belief that Jesus, the Christ, is exalted to the highest place of honour in the very centre of the universe as the conclusion of his work as the Saviour of mankind. This is a point to which we shall return later.

However, taking for granted this special way in which the writers of both the New Testament and theology use language of the exalted Christ we must go on to affirm that there is much information about the life of the exalted Christ in the New Testament of which we can learn and which can nourish our faith. This information and teaching, having been written from within Christian faith and commitment, and having been inspired by the Holy Spirit, can only be truly understood and appreciated by those who have put on, by obeying the Gospel, the spectacles of faith. It is written from faith to faith. Therefore to the non-Christian the whole idea of the human life of the Son of God existing and being lived in heaven for thousands of years is probably without meaning or importance.

The creeds of Christendom say little about this heavenly life of the exalted Saviour; they merely state the fact of it. In the Nicene Creed we say, 'He ascended into heaven and is seated at the right hand of the Father. He will come again in glory to judge the living and the dead, and his kingdom will have no end.' The Apostles' Creed is virtually the same and we say, 'He ascended into heaven, and is seated at the right hand of the Father. He will come again to judge the living and the dead.'

It is not always noticed that the fact of the Ascension of Christ Jesus was an ingredient of the first sermon of the Church, preached by Peter on the day of Pentecost: 'This Jesus ... has been raised to the right-hand side of God, his Father, and has received from him the Holy Spirit, as he had promised' (Acts 2:32–3). This gift of the Spirit was for the Church so that Jesus Christ could be spiritually active, known and loved within the community of God's people.

The relation between the Resurrection and Ascension

How do we relate the Resurrection and the Ascension? The testimony of the four Gospels is that Jesus of Nazareth died, was buried, and on the third day returned to life. His complete body—not merely his human soul or his divine nature—came back to life so that all that was left in the rock-tomb where he was placed on the Good Friday was the linen cloth in which his body had been wrapped. As the resurrected Jesus, he was seen and eventually recognised by his disciples; some of them ate with him and others walked with him. Though his body was recognised as being that which he had before the Crucifixion, it was no longer subject to the restrictions of time and space as it had been previously. So we read that Jesus passed through doors without opening them (John 20:19, 26-8) and was able to disappear after holding a conversation (Luke 24:31). The only satisfactory way to relate the Resurrection and Ascension to each other is to say that they are two parts of one great action of God. The action is the exaltation of Jesus the Christ to the spiritual centre of the universe, that is into heaven to the right hand side of the Father. This is beautifully expressed in the hymn of Philippians, chapter 2, verses 6-11.

> He always had the nature of God,
> > but he did not think that by force he should try to become equal with God.
>
> Instead of this, of his own free will he gave up all he had
> > and took the nature of a servant.
>
> He became like man
> > and appeared in human likeness.
>
> He was humble and walked the path of obedience all the way to death—his death on the cross.
>
> For this reason God raised him to the highest place above
> > and gave him the name that is greater than any other name.
>
> And so, in honour of the name of Jesus
> > all beings in heaven, on earth and in the world below will fall on their knees
>
> and all will openly proclaim that Jesus Christ is Lord, to the glory of God the Father.

Peter also taught that the exaltation was from Hades (the

sphere of death) to the right hand of God (1 Pet. 3:18–22). As the hymnwriter Thomas Kelly expressed it:

> *The head that once was crowned with thorns,*
> *Is crowned with glory now:*
> *A royal diadem adorns*
> *The mighty Victor's brow.*
>
> *The highest place that heaven affords*
> *Is his, is his by right,*
> *The King of kings, and Lord of lords,*
> *And heaven's eternal light.*

From the horrible death of crucifixion and the descent into Hades Jesus went triumphantly into the courts of heaven after his body had been raised from the dead.

The ascension of Christ to 'the highest place that heaven affords' was not postponed, however, until the fortieth day after the Resurrection. Rather, he probably ascended late on the evening of the day on which he rose. As this statement may come as a surprise to some people a few explanatory comments are needed. Much of our thinking about the time of the Ascension has been dominated by the account in Acts chapter 1 verses 1–11 in which we are told that 'for forty days after his death he appeared to them many times in ways that proved beyond doubt that he was alive'. The Church Year, building on this period of forty days, placed Ascension Day exactly forty days after Easter Day. Therefore for many of us this period of forty days has become sacrosanct even though we are aware that the number forty, against the Old Testament background, is very often a symbolic number and is not intended to be interpreted chronologically. If we do believe that Jesus rose from the dead on the Sunday and then forty days later ascended into heaven we have to face such questions as: 'Where was Jesus when he was not appearing to his disciples?' and 'Was he invisibly present with them all the time and only became visible to them at specific moments?'

Now if we only had Acts chapter 1 to guide our thinking we would probably have to find answers to these questions. Yet even if we did another question would arise, and it would be this. According to Acts chapter 1 the resurrection appearances of Jesus ceased on the fortieth day with the Ascension, but according to Paul in 1 Corinthians 15:8 the risen Jesus also appeared to him in the same way in which he appeared to Peter and James and others. Thus the description of Paul's experience of the risen Jesus on the road to Damascus (Acts chapter 9) does appear to be in conflict with Luke's apparent claim that the resurrection appearances ceased on the fortieth day.

But if we leave the Acts and turn to the Gospels then we can see in them the possibility of the Ascension having taken place on the first Sunday. First of all, Luke himself appears to describe the Ascension as taking place at the end of the same Sunday when Jesus walked to Emmaus with the two disciples. 'Then he led them out of the city as far as Bethany, where he raised his hands and blessed them. As he was blessing them, he departed from them and was taken up into heaven. They worshipped him and went back into Jerusalem, filled with great joy, and spent all their time in the Temple giving thanks to God' (Luke 24:50-52).

Secondly, Mark also appears to understand the Ascension as taking place at the end of the Sunday on which

Jesus had risen from death. 'After the Lord Jesus had talked with them, he was taken up to heaven and sat at the right side of God' (Mark 16:19).

Thirdly, Matthew may well be describing not the Ascension but rather a visitation by the ascended Jesus, when he relates that Jesus met the disciples in Galilee and said to them, 'I have been given all authority in heaven and on earth' (Matt. 28:18). It is only after the entrance into heaven and the coronation there that Jesus is given the title of 'King of kings' so that all power belongs to him.

Fourthly, while the Gospel of John contains no description of the Ascension it does describe the visit of the risen Jesus to the disciples when the words 'Receive the Holy Spirit' were spoken by him (John 20:22). Now in John's Gospel the gift of the Spirit is related to the glorification (exaltation) of Jesus and so this passage where Jesus gives the Spirit would best fit into an understanding of the Ascension as taking place on the Sunday evening. That this was John's understanding is strengthened by the way in which Jesus spoke to Mary. When he met her in the garden he did not say 'I shall ascend' but 'I am ascending', that is, he was in the process of 'returning to him' who is Father Almighty (John 20:17).

If Jesus ascended into heaven on the evening of the Sunday, then what we call the resurrection appearances can be understood as short periods, in time and space, when the glorified Jesus condescended to the temporal and material conditions which he had fully known from the time of his birth in Bethlehem until his resurrection. He entered again into time and space from the eternal world not to prove to the world that he had overcome death but to encourage his disciples and prepare them for both his final withdrawal from them and the coming, in his place and name, of the Holy Spirit.

It would appear that if a living being is not conditioned by time and space then that being is either in the presence of God or in the presence of Satan and the fallen angels. Jesus, resurrected from the dead, was certainly not conditioned either by human or spatial limitations. This is evident from the description in the Gospels of the resurrection appearances. Now this means that if his rightful or natural place was no longer in the created universe of time and space then it was in the sphere we may call the spiritual or the supernatural. Obviously, as it was not with Satan and his hosts, it must have been with God in heaven.

Yet the resurrected Jesus was the Servant of God, the Saviour of the world, and it was his task to create a new humanity, a community redeemed by his sacrificial death. So, in order to demonstrate his victory over death to those who would be the major leaders of this new community, he freely chose to accommodate himself to the limitations of human sense experience for most of the first day after his resurrection. By showing himself alive he declared to the disciples that he was the conqueror of death and the Lord of life.

It was only after the truth of the Resurrection had begun to be assimilated by the disciples that Jesus led them to the hill from which he made what we call his ascension. From the viewpoint of heaven Jesus, Son of God, had already been restored to his rightful place in heaven from the moment of his resurrection. But, accommodating himself to the needs and framework of thought of his disciples, Jesus did not demonstrate the truth of his exaltation until the reality of the Resurrection was appreciated by them. Thus from the hill in Bethany, in a manner which men who read the Old Testament would understand, Jesus left the earth for heaven. No doubt if the cosmological viewpoint of the disciples had been that of modern educated scientists then Jesus would have demonstrated his victory over death and his entrance into the glory of God in a way that they would find convincing.

But, if this is so, it is rightly asked why Luke insists on the forty days of resurrection appearances with the climax of the Ascension. The answer is probably to be sought in the fact that Luke apparently modelled his account of the Ascension on the story of Elijah's ascension. According to 2 Kings 2 Elijah is taken up to heaven while Elisha, his servant, remains behind awaiting the gift of the Spirit of God. Into this model Luke has imported the symbolical forty days, the number forty being known to all readers of the Old Testament as a number with special significance (see Exod. 16:35; Num. 14:33; Judg. 3:11, 13:1; Ps. 95:10; Ezek. 29:11, etc.). An interesting further dimension to this use of the symbolic forty is that in contemporary Jewish literature there are references to ascension into heaven after forty days. In the Apocalypse of Baruch there is a scribe who waits upon a mountain for forty days before being lifted up to heaven (76:4) and in The Second Book of Esdras it is written of Ezra that he spent forty days copying out the Torah (the law of God) before he was taken up into heaven (14:9, 23, 44).[1]

Not all our problems are solved by this reconstruction but at least it does fit into the theology of Paul for whom Christ was lifted out of Hades to the right hand of God, out of the abyss where Satan rules, through Resurrection and Ascension to the position of Lord of the universe (Rom. 10:6–7; Eph. 4:7–10).[2]

Returning to Acts chapter 1 verse 9 we read that Jesus 'was taken up to heaven as they watched him, and a cloud hid him from their sight'. The cloud reminds us of what happened a year or so earlier on the mountain in Galilee when Jesus was transfigured before three of his disciples. The cloud which covered Jesus and from which came the voice from heaven declaring Jesus to be the Son of God (Luke 9:28–36) was the *Shekinah*, the manifestation of the glory of God. The *Shekinah* was a glowing cloud which was the sign of God's holy presence. *Shekinah* is not a biblical word but a rabbinic word and is a synonym for the 'pillar of cloud' which used to descend upon the ancient Tabernacle when the Lord wished to speak to Moses (Exod. 33:7–11). It is also the name of the cloud which filled the new Temple built by Solomon when it was dedicated (1 Kgs. 8). It was into this *Shekinah* that Jesus disappeared as he went from the earth. By this dramatic symbolism Luke is teaching that Jesus ascended into the presence and glory of God; when next he made a universal appearance on earth it would be in the same glory to be the Judge of the nations.

It is sometimes said that because the description of the Ascension is bound up with pre-Copernican views of the universe, that is a flat world with heaven up in the skies, and because ancient cosmological views of the universe are now totally discredited, so also is the ascension of Jesus Christ. Such a charge is only valid if we cling to a three-decker universe with hell beneath us and heaven above us. The Hebrew mind, unlike that of the Greek, knew of no natural sciences or physics. It did not look upon the world as a closed system which could be measured by mathematics and whose laws could be known. Rather, the world belonged to God and it was the scene of God's encounter with man. Anyone leaving the surface of the earth must appear to spectators to be 'going up' and thus the spectators must look upwards. The fact that someone appears to go upwards is not necessarily another way of saying that heaven is simply 'up there'. Jesus went from one mode of existence to another in his ascension, from the material world to the spiritual world, from the natural world to the supernatural world, from the finite world to the infinite world, from earth to heaven. The presence of the *Shekinah* guaranteed this!

A PRAYER

O God our Father, we praise you that for our sake your Son took human nature and lived as the man, Jesus of Nazareth. We give you hearty thanks that he lived a perfect life of obedience to your will and then gave himself in death that we might receive the forgiveness of sins and your grace. We also thank you that you raised him from the grave and the power of death and exalted him to be the Lord of heaven and earth. Grant us your help so that we shall ever treat him as Lord, for in his name we pray. Amen.

NOTES

[1] See further F. F. Bruce, *Commentary on the Book of Acts* (1965), pp. 30ff.
[2] For the view that the Resurrection was also the Ascension and that what is usually called the Ascension is merely the end of the resurrection appearances see G. E. Ladd, *I Believe in the Resurrection of Jesus* (1975), pp. 126–9.

3 Jesus, Messiah and Lord

THE WRITERS OF the New Testament, followed by the ancient Creeds, saw two parts to the ascension of Christ into the glory of God in heaven. First of all they tell us that 'he was taken up to heaven'; and, secondly, that 'he sat at the right side of God' (Mark 16:19). Let us take these two aspects in turn.

Jesus enters heaven

The Ascension, as we have seen, was a withdrawal once for all from the whole order of existence which men live on this side of death and the grave. It was a removal from our world of sense experience. The 'going up' of Jesus into heaven was also, at the same time, his being 'taken up'. Put another way the Ascension was also an Assumption, and the two ideas are complementary. Jesus entered the presence of God, the Father Almighty, in his own right as the Son of God; also, as the Obedient Man, he was exalted to heaven as a reward for his perfect obedience to the will of God the Father. There are two Old Testament passages which have traditionally been used in the liturgy of the Western Church for Ascension Day and they help to convey these two ideas.

There is Psalm 24. This was used within Israel in the procession to the Temple at a major festival. As the worshippers walk up the hill of Zion in Jerusalem they sing:

> Who has the right to go up the Lord's hill?
>> Who may enter his holy Temple?
> Those who are pure in act and in thought,
>> who do not worship idols or make false promises.
> The Lord will bless them and save them;
>> God will declare them innocent.
> Such are the people who come to God,
>> who come into the presence of the God of Jacob.

At the gates of the Temple the procession halts and the people cry:

> Fling wide the gates,
>> open the ancient doors,
>> and the great king will come in.

From inside the gates the Levites ask:

> Who is this great king?

To this the people respond:

> He is the Lord, strong and mighty,
>> the Lord, victorious in battle.
> Fling wide the gates,
>> open the ancient doors,
>> and the great king will come in.

Again the Levites ask:

> Who is this great king?

The answer returns:

> The triumphant Lord—he is the great king!

So the procession of the triumphant Lord enters into the Temple courts.

It is easy to see how the early Church related this psalm to Jesus. As there was an ascent up Mount Zion and then an entry into the courts of the Temple, so Jesus ascended into the heavenly Temple which is heaven. Then, as in the psalm the Lord Jehovah (*Yahweh*) through his servant the king is depicted as triumphant over his enemies, so Jesus was triumphant over the forces of evil and death and entered heaven as the great conqueror. It was thoughts such as these which inspired Bishop Christopher Wordsworth of Lincoln to write the following hymn:

See the Conqueror mounts in triumph; see the King in royal state,
Riding on the clouds his chariot to his heavenly palace gate;
Hark the choirs of angel voices joyful Alleluias sing,
And the portals high are lifted up to receive their heavenly King.

Who is this that comes in glory, with the trump of jubilee?
Lord of battles, God of armies, he has gained the victory;
He who on the cross did suffer, he who from the grave arose,
He has vanquished sin and Satan, he by death has spoiled his foes.

He has raised our human nature on the clouds to God's right hand,
There we sit in heavenly places, there with him in glory stand:
Jesus reigns, adored by angels; Man with God is on the throne;
Mighty Lord, in thine ascension, we by faith behold our own.

Glory be to God the Father; glory be to God the Son,
Dying, risen, ascending for us, who the heavenly realm has won;
Glory to the Holy Spirit; to One God in Persons Three,
Glory both in earth and heaven, glory, endless glory be.

Because Jesus was the perfectly obedient Man in word and in thought he was raised by God the Father to his right hand on high, there to be worshipped by angels.

The second passage is 2 Kings 2. When 'the time came for the Lord to take Elijah up to heaven in a whirlwind' the prophet, sensing that his end was near determined to visit for the last time the hills of his native Gilead. On his way there he desired to visit ancient sanctuaries where schools of the prophets were established. He was accompanied by Elisha who had been with him for ten years. They went to Gilgal and then to Bethel. Elisha refused to leave Elijah although the latter begged him to stay at Gilgal. At Bethel the youthful prophets told Elisha that the Lord was about to take away his master but he refused to discuss the matter with them even as he refused to listen to Elijah when he once more begged him to stay in the town. They proceeded to the river Jordan. Conscious that some great event was impending, fifty of the young men from the prophetic school watched the two men as they entered the river valley and approached the water. Elijah took off his cloak, rolled it up and struck the water with it. The water divided and the two men crossed. On reaching the other side Elisha told Elijah that above all things he wished to be his master's successor as the prophet of the Lord who was empowered by the Spirit of the Lord. Elijah replied saying that what he asked was a great request but that if he remained his prayer would be granted. 'They kept talking as they walked on; then suddenly a chariot of fire pulled by horses of fire came between them and Elijah was taken up to heaven by a whirlwind' (verse 11). Elisha was overcome with grief and amazement, but his prayer was granted and he received the power of the Spirit of the Lord.

As Elijah was the unparalleled champion for the honour of the Lord, a fiery chariot was the symbol of his triumphal procession into heaven. Jesus, likewise the champion of the honour of the Lord, but also the conqueror of death, ascended to the Father, a cloud receiving him out of the sight of his disciples who, like Elisha, received the Spirit which had filled their Master.

Jesus sits at God's right hand

Secondly, the Ascension led to what is often called the Session—the sitting at the right hand of the Father. This expression occurs several times in the New Testament (e.g. Mark 14:62; Eph. 1:20-1; Col. 3:1; Heb. 1:3, 8:1, 12:2 and 1 Pet. 3:22) and it is taken from Psalm 110. The general thought behind this psalm and others (e.g. Pss. 2 and 45) is that while God is enthroned over the world in general and Israel in particular David or the king of Israel is for the time being his vicegerent.

The Lord said to my lord, the king,
  'Sit here at my right
  until I put your enemies under your feet.'
From Zion the Lord will extend your royal power.
  'Rule over your enemies', he says.

On the day you fight your enemies,
   your people will volunteer.
Like the dew of early morning
   your young men will come to you on the sacred hills.

The Lord made a solemn promise and will not take it back:
   'You will be a priest for ever
   in the line of succession to Melchizedek.'

The Lord is at your right side;
   when he becomes angry, he will defeat kings.
He will pass judgment on the nations
   and fill the battlefield with corpses;
   he will defeat kings all over the earth.
The king will drink from the stream by the road,
   and strengthened, he will stand victorious.

Here we have the coronation of the king as the representative of God and God's righteous reign; his investiture with the sceptre of power; the joyful homage of his people; the oath of God concerning him 'for ever' (that is, with his successors) in the Melchizedek priesthood in Zion; his victory over the kings and nations who are opposed to the God of Israel, and his spiritual refreshment. In the week which we call Passion Week Jesus had this psalm in mind. The questions which he put to the crowd in the Temple about the Messiah being a descendant of David were based on the contents of this psalm and Jesus actually quoted from it (Mark 12:35-7; Matt. 22:41-6; Luke 20:41-4). So from Jesus himself the apostles learned to see in this coronation psalm a prophecy of his ascension and kingly rule and as we shall see later the writer of the Epistle to the Hebrews developed from it his doctrine of Jesus as the fulfilment of the Melchizedek priesthood. The psalm was quoted by Peter on the Day of Pentecost (Acts 2:34–5) and is either directly or indirectly used in ten or more other passages (Acts 7:55–6; Rom. 8:34; Eph. 1:20; Col. 3:1; Heb. 1:3,13, 8:1, 10:12, 12:2; 1 Pet. 3:22; Rev. 3:21, 12:5).

By the use of this psalm, especially the opening verse, Christians were led to think of Jesus as invested with the highest honour of which humanity is capable under God. Also they were led to think of him as the Representative or Viceroy of the Father who is certain to triumph ultimately over all that is opposed to him. So 'we see him now crowned with glory and honour because of the death he suffered' (Heb. 2:9) and there in heaven 'he now waits until God puts his enemies as a footstool under his feet' (Heb. 10:13). It was noted in chapter two that the picture of the throne and of Jesus sitting upon it is the language of symbolism not of (in the normal sense of the words) historical fact. Through the picture we learn that all power and authority in the universe is given by the Father to the exalted Jesus and therefore we know that his plan and purpose for the human race will be sure ultimately to triumph. Death, sin and evil will at the end of the present age be as surely vanquished as, in our daily experience, the darkness of night is dispelled by the light of dawn.

The idea conveyed by the sitting upon the throne is that of ruling over the world and waiting until the time appointed by the Father arrives for the exalted God-Man to go forth and execute the final victory in God's name upon earth and in the whole universe. In his vision Stephen the martyr saw 'the Son of Man standing at the right-hand side of God' (Acts 7:56, cf. Rev. 5:6). Here, the idea is probably that of the readiness of the exalted Jesus to return to earth in order to judge the nations. It is interesting to note that the Apostles' and Nicene Creeds have both followed the powerful imagery of 'sitting' taken from Psalm 110 instead of the idea of standing.

It was, of course, on the basis of the exaltation that the apostles proclaimed Jesus of Nazareth as the Messiah, the King and the Lord. Peter preached that 'this Jesus, whom you [Jews] crucified, is the one that God has made Lord and Messiah' (Acts 2:36). Later he declared that 'the God of our ancestors raised Jesus from death . . . God raised him to his right-hand side as Leader [Prince] and Saviour, to give the people of Israel the opportunity to repent and have their sins forgiven' (Acts 5:30–1). John, the Seer of Patmos, heard angels, thousands and millions of them, joining with others in singing of Jesus the King:

> The Lamb who was killed is worthy
> to receive power, wealth, wisdom, and strength,
> honour, glory, and praise! (Rev. 5:12)

By the Resurrection and Ascension Jesus of Nazareth was vindicated by God and declared to be the long-expected Jewish Messiah. Also he was appointed by the Father to be the Ruler of the whole world until the end of the age, when the totally new order of 'new heavens and new earth' would come into being. Thus the name which 'is greater than any other name' of which Paul speaks in Philippians 2:9 is the name 'Lord'. At the end of the present evil age 'all will openly proclaim that Jesus Christ is Lord to the glory of God the Father'.

It will perhaps help the development of our thinking in later chapters if we spend a little time here explaining in fairly general terms the meaning of the three titles Messiah, King and Lord.

Jesus, the Messiah

Our word 'Christ' comes to us via the Latin word *Christus*, itself from the Greek *Christos*, which in the Greek version of the Old Testament (the Septuagint) translated the Hebrew word *Messiah*, that is, the anointed one of God. From the Old Testament we learn of two divinely ordained office bearers who were anointed with oil, the high priest (Exod. 28:41, 30:30) and the king (1 Sam. 15:1). Kings were often termed 'the Anointed of God'. For example, in Psalm 20 verse 6 the psalmist confidently sings, 'Now I know the Lord will help his anointed' (cf. Pss. 18:50, 28:8, 84:9, 89:38,51, 132:10,17RSV).

The hope of a future Messiah who would be God's agent as saviour and deliverer of the whole people was particularly associated with a man who would be a direct descendant of David. Through Jeremiah God said, 'The time is coming when I will choose as king a righteous descendant of David. That king will rule wisely and do what is right and just throughout the land. When he is king, the people of Judah will be safe, and the people of Israel will live in peace. He will be called "the Lord Our Salvation"' (23:5–6).

Through Ezekiel God also said, 'I will give them a king like my servant David to be their one shepherd, and he will take care of them. I, the Lord, will be their God, and a king like my servant David will be their ruler' (34:23–4).

The coming Messiah-King was also called 'Son' by God. There is the familiar passage in Psalm 2 verses 7–9:

'I will announce,' says the king, 'What the Lord has declared.
  He said to me: "You are my son;
  today I have become your father.
Ask, and I will give you all the nations;
  the whole earth will be yours.
You will break them with an iron rod;
  you will shatter them in pieces like a clay pot."'

Whether we are right—in terms of Old Testament theology—to identify the Messiah-King, who is 'Son of God', with the Suffering Servant of Isaiah (42:1ff., 49:1ff., 50:4ff., 52:13–53:12) is not easy to answer for scholars are not in agreement. It is possible that in Isaiah's thought the Servant was the whole Israel or a righteous remnant of the people. However, Jesus of Nazareth certainly appears to have identified himself as fulfilling to some extent the role of the Servant who suffers and is vindicated finally by God. He said: 'For even the Son of Man did not come to be served; he came to serve and to give his life to redeem many people' (Mark 10:45; see also Matt. 18–21; Luke 22:37). (As is apparent from this quotation the favourite term of Jesus to describe himself was that of 'Son of Man', a term which could mean 'a man' or if Daniel 7 is taken into account could mean a man who is exalted to the throne of God.)

In the Synoptic Gospels the title Messiah is not used by Jesus of himself except in special circumstances. He accepted the confession of Peter, 'You are the Messiah' (Mark 8:29) but directed Peter and the disciples to think not in terms of an earthly, kingly rule but rather of a Servant who suffered for the people. He also accepted the title when he was questioned by the High Priest (Mark 14:61–2) but again invited the hearers to consider the nature of messiahship by teaching concerning the Son of Man (verse 62).

Even if Jesus did not make use of the title, all the Gospels were written from the conviction that he was the promised 'Anointed One', the descendant of David (Luke 1:69, 2:4; Matt. 9:27, 15:22; John 1:45). The apostolic message which we find in the sermons of the Acts proceeded on this assumption (Acts 3:18 etc.) as did the teaching of Paul (Rom. 1:3; 1 Cor. 15:1–7).

A remarkable aspect of the New Testament portrayal of Jesus as Messiah is that the writers find no contradiction between his violent death upon the Cross and his title of Messiah. Contemporary Jewish thought could not begin to entertain the idea of the Messiah-King suffering, let alone dying the ignominious death of a criminal upon a cross erected by imperial Rome. Finding inspiration from the Servant passages of Isaiah the apostles declared that what happened in the Passion of Jesus was according to the plan of God. Peter declared: 'In accordance with his own plan God had already decided that Jesus would be handed over to you ; and you killed him by letting sinful men crucify him. But God raised him from death, setting him free from its power' (Acts 2:23–4).

It is perhaps worth adding that the original use of the term Messiah in Hebrew is adjectival—the 'anointed' priest or the 'anointed' king. In the Greek-speaking churches the term *Christos* functioned as a proper name, being linked with 'Jesus' as 'Jesus Christ' or 'Christ Jesus'. Happily this change did not detract from the idea of majesty and so to call Jesus of Nazareth 'Jesus Christ' was to confess that Jesus of Nazareth had been declared by God to be King and Saviour of both Jews and Gentiles.

Jesus, the King

In the Old Testament the God of Israel is often called 'the King' or is said to reign as King over the world. Describing his vision of God Isaiah claimed that with his own eyes he had 'seen the King, the Lord Almighty' (6:5). Later he referred to 'the Lord, the King of Israel' (41:21) and to 'the Lord, who rules and protects Israel' (44:6). Then, looking forward to God's final vindication and salvation of his people, he wrote, 'How wonderful it is to see a messenger coming across the mountains, bringing good news, the news of peace! He announces victory and says to Zion, "Your God is King!"' (52:7).

As he rules both Israel and the nations of the whole world, Yahweh is truly King (cf. Jer. 10:7; Pss. 47:3, 99:2, 110:2-6).

In the Gospels, especially in the description of the trial before the Roman Procurator Pilate, Jesus is portrayed as the King (Greek *basileus*) of the Jews and of the world. The thought here, from the Jewish side, is that of the messianic king, whom the Pharisees and Sadducees could not believe Jesus to be; but, from the Roman side the king is seen only in wordly terms. Pilate asked Jesus, 'Are you the king of the Jews?' To which Jesus gave an indirect answer (Mark 15:2; Matt. 27:11; Luke 23:3). Later the soldiers mocked him saying, 'Long live the King of the Jews!' (Mark 15:18; Matt. 27:29) and on the Cross the Romans placed the inscription, 'The King of the Jews' (Mark 15:26; Matt. 27:37; Luke 23:38; John 19:19), written in Hebrew, Greek and Latin. The three languages signified for Christians that the crucified One was Jesus the universal King. As Jesus hung on the Cross he was mocked by those who passed by as they said, 'Let us see the Messiah, the king of Israel, come down from the cross now, and we will believe him!' (Mark 15:32; Matt. 27:42; Luke 23:35).

Outside the four Gospels there is no mention of the titles 'King of Israel' and 'King of the Jews'. However, the idea of Jesus, the *basileus*, lies behind such a passage as Acts chapter 17 verse 7. Here, in the middle of an account of the accusation brought by Jews against Paul and Silas, who were making converts from the Jewish synagogue, come the words, 'They are all breaking the laws of the Emperor, saying that there is another king, whose name is Jesus'. Paul, as we shall see below, made use of the word 'Lord' instead of 'King' in the development of his theology of the exalted Jesus. Even so he did make use of the expression 'the Kingdom of Christ' (Eph. 5:5) and speaking of the final resurrection of the dead at the end of the age he wrote of the exalted Jesus handing over the kingdom to his Father at the end of the age (1 Cor. 15:23-5). Then also in Romans chapter 5 verses 12-21 Paul spoke of grace reigning 'through righteousness to eternal life through Jesus Christ our Lord' (RSV). The use of the verb 'to reign' five times in this passage reminds the reader of the gracious rule of Jesus the King of righteousness and salvation.

John on Patmos was more explicit because the historical circumstances in which he wrote were different. The Emperor Nero had already begun to cause the blood of the martyrs to flow (AD 64) and Domitian (AD 90) appeared to be about to inaugurate a widespread persecution of those who would not openly proclaim that he, the Emperor, was 'Lord and God'. The time had come for Christians to accept the challenge. Therefore Jesus Christ is declared by John to be 'the ruler of the kings of the world'; he is 'King of kings and Lord of lords' and with his elect he will reign for a thousand years, and eventually the kingdoms of this world will become the kingdom of God and of his Christ (Rev. 1:5, 19:16, 20:4, 11:15). In John's theology the ascended Jesus is the King above the Emperor, the true Ruler of the world.

Jesus, the Lord

The Greek word *kyrios*, which we usually translate 'Master' or 'Lord', occurs in some 717 passages in the New Testament and of these 210 are in Luke's writings and 275 in Paul's epistles. Significantly both these authors had a Greek-speaking audience in mind and *kyrios* was a word with which such people were familiar. Not in all the occasions when *kyrios* is used does it refer to God or to the Lord Jesus Christ, for the word was used to describe anyone who had an authority of one kind or another. For example in Luke 16:3,5 *kyrios* is the rich owner of property and slaves while in Ephesians 6:5,9 the *kyrios* is firstly the owner of the Christian slave and secondly the Christian slave-owner. Peter used the word to describe the husband in his relationship to his wife, stating that 'Sarah ... obeyed Abraham and called him her master' (1 Pet. 3:6). This general use of *kyrios* harmonises with the use of the word in the Greek version of the Old Testament, the Septuagint, where the word occurs over 9,000 times and is used both of the Lordship of God and the varied types of rule within human society.

Kyrios, however, is certainly used in the New Testament of the God who is the creator and ruler of the whole universe. In Luke's account of the preparation for the birth of Jesus, the angel tells Mary that she will have a son who 'will be great and will be called the Son of the Most High God'. This 'Most High God' is then called 'the *Lord*' who will make Jesus into a king (1:32). When Paul is describing the faith of Abraham he makes use of a quotation from Psalm 32 which reads, 'Happy is the person whose sins the *Lord* will not keep account of' (Rom. 4:8). The 'Lord' here is the God of Israel, the God who created heaven and earth. Turning to the last chapter of the last book of the Bible we find the angel telling John that the words he has heard he can surely trust for 'the *Lord* God who gives his Spirit to the prophets has sent his angel' (Rev. 22.6) as the guarantee of truth.

Kyrios is used of Jesus of Nazareth, the Christ, in different ways. First of all in the Gospels, that is in the period of his earthly ministry, he was called *kyrios* by people who were using the term as a synonym for Rabbi, a respected Jewish teacher of the Law. At the transfiguration of Jesus Matthew records that Peter said to Jesus, '*Kyrios*, how good it is that we are here' (Matt. 17:4); in the parallel account in Mark 9:5 Jesus is called 'Rabbi' or 'Teacher' and in Luke 9:33 'Master' (translating yet another Greek word). This shows that 'Lord' and 'Rabbi' could be synonyms. Some people who heard Jesus teach were impressed by his authority and thus called him 'Lord' but in Luke 6:46–9 Jesus is portrayed as being impatient with those who called him Lord but did not act upon his authoritative words (cf. Matt. 7:24–7).

Following the ascension of Jesus we find that the word *kyrios* takes on a large new dimension of meaning and holds within itself the key to the way in which the Greek-speaking Christian community now viewed the exalted Jesus. The confession of faith, 'Jesus is Lord', was a summary for them of the heart of what was Christianity. Obviously 'Lord' here meant much more than 'Jewish teacher' or 'a human being possessing gifts of leadership'. Having been exalted to the heart of heaven Jesus the Christ was now the Ruler of the universe; he was the King of the kings, the One who had been set above all the angelic and demonic powers. In the Aramaic-speaking churches of Palestine the thought of Jesus as Lord was conveyed in the cry, '*Maranatha*' (1 Cor. 16:22) which meant 'Come Lord'. The churches which used Greek were led by the apostles, Paul in particular, to speak of the reign of the exalted Jesus as the reign of the *kyrios*. A common word, it was used of such gods as Isis, Osiris and Serapis and was also used of the Roman Emperor in the eastern half of the Empire. Thus Paul can speak of 'gods many and lords many' in pagan religion and society, but for him there is the 'one God ... and one Lord Jesus Christ' (1 Cor. 8:5–6).

So they came to call the One who had taken his assumed humanity into heaven (having in and through that humanity earned for man the gift of eternal life) 'Lord'. Because Yahweh was called 'Lord' in the Greek Bible, this term conveyed the idea of his deity as eternal Son of God; and because certain human beings were called 'lord' the term also conveyed the idea of the exaltation of his assumed human nature to the spiritual centre of the universe, to the place of all final power and authority. Therefore the usual way of describing Jesus of

Nazareth, the Saviour of Jews and Gentiles, quickly came to be 'the Lord Jesus Christ', an expression which is often used in the greetings which appear at the beginning of the epistles of the New Testament.

As time went by, and as the apostles meditated upon the exaltation and coronation of Jesus in heaven they came, by the inspiration of the Holy Spirit, to see and to develop various aspects of this role of Jesus as *kyrios*. They came to see his relation to the creation and the preservation of the cosmos, to the history of the nations and their rulers, to the churches, to the individual Christian and to the end of the age. They also came to use the term *kyrios* in relation to specific Christian ordinances and institutions of the churches—for example, the Lord's Day (Rev. 1:10) and the Lord's Supper (1 Cor. 11:20). To these two, later Christians added a third 'The Lord's Prayer'. The Lord's Day was the commemoration each Sunday of the day when the glorious resurrection of Jesus, the Lord, took place. The Lord's Supper was both the commemoration of the sacrificial death of Jesus and the sitting down in his presence (through the Spirit) to be fed spiritually.

A PRAYER

O God, our Father, we have joyfully confessed with heart and voice that 'Jesus Christ is Lord'. We believe that he is exalted far above all earthly and demonic powers and that now from heaven he rules for your glory over the universe, the history of nations and especially over the Church, which he purchased by his sacrificial death. Teach us always to remember the glorious fact of his exaltation and to live in the light of it, for in his exalted name we pray. Amen.

4 The meaning of the Ascension

IN THE LAST two chapters we used a variety of material from the New Testament in order to give a general introduction to the apostolic understanding of the exaltation of Jesus. Here, following the contemporary trend to speak of specific theologies within the Bible (e.g. a Pauline and a Lucan theology) our task is to note the complementary theologies of the ascension of Jesus. In doing this it may be helpful to think of the different insights and interpretations developed by the different writers as one thinks of the colours of the rainbow, different but complementary, and all together making the complete interpretation. Together with our study of the words King, Messiah and Lord, this theology will help us to understand the doctrine of Christ as Lord of the cosmos, of history and of the Church.

Matthew's teaching

One of the main themes of this Gospel is that of the kingdom of heaven. Thus the Ascension is viewed as the enthronement of the Messiah as the King of kings. To him is given all authority in heaven and on earth and therefore he sends out his disciples to make converts from among the nations of the world (28:18–20). In the background here is the teaching from Daniel 7:14 where the Son of Man is given 'authority, honour and royal power, so that the people of all nations, races and languages would serve him'. The kingdom of the ascended Messiah is both the community of disciples and the whole world. Matthew also makes it clear that the gift of the Spirit to the disciples and to the world is linked with the ascension of Jesus. This is implicit in the words describing the baptism of Jesus. As he *came up* from the water 'heaven was opened to him' and he saw the Spirit of God descending to him. At the same time the voice from heaven declared that ' "This is my own dear Son" ' (3:16–17). As he ascended from the water, heaven opened and the Spirit descended upon him. So later, heaven opened for him to ascend, and for the Spirit to come to the disciples.

It is probable that the parable of the three servants (25:14–30) also refers to the Ascension. The merchant who goes to a distant place leaving his servants to administer his property can be understood as the going of Jesus up into heaven. The return of the merchant to settle accounts can then be taken to refer to the Second Coming of the now exalted Jesus in order to judge the nations.

Mark's teaching

According to Mark Jesus told the High Priest and the Sanhedrin that they would 'all see the Son of Man seated on the right of the Almighty and coming with the clouds of heaven' (14:62). This may be a reference to the second coming of the Lord Jesus; more probably, following Psalm 110 and Daniel 7, it is a reference to the triumphal entry of the resurrected Jesus into the courts of heaven to be enthroned as Messiah-King and to prepare the way for his people, who would follow him. Then would occur the Second Coming. That the position of Jesus after the Ascension will be one of glory is made clear in several places (8:38, 13:26, 16:19). As in Matthew the description of the baptism of Jesus (1:10) links his glorification with the coming of the Spirit, the same Spirit in whose power 'the disciples went and preached everywhere, and the Lord worked with them and proved their preaching was true by the miracles that were performed' (16:20).

Luke's teaching

For Luke the Ascension (Luke 24:50–51; Acts 1:1–12) is nothing less than the reversal by God of the verdict passed by sinful man upon Jesus of Nazareth. The Jews and Romans put him to death as a common criminal but God raised him from the dead 'setting him free from its power because it was impossible that death should hold him prisoner' (Acts 2:24). God raised him to his own right-hand side, declaring him to be the Messiah (2:32–4). Therefore Jesus is now the 'Lord of all' (10:36). It is the case that the 'God of Abraham, Isaac and Jacob, the God of our ancestors, has given divine glory to his Servant, Jesus' (3:13) so that as Jesus promised, he could send from the heavenly glory the gift of the Holy Spirit to the Church (2:33). This gift was received on the Day of Pentecost and became the life-giving reality in the work of the apostles and experience of the Christians.

Most scholars believe that for Luke there was a close connection between the transfiguration (Luke 9:28–36) and the ascension of Jesus (Acts 1), the former being a prefigurement of the latter. In the former Jesus entered into the *Shekinah* but he did not remain in the cloud for his mission was not yet completed. At his ascension Jesus entered once more into the *Shekinah* and this time he did not return. Thus the Ascension is seen by Luke as the final parting, ending both the messianic mission and the resurrection appearances. In this connection it is significant that after his description of the Transfiguration Luke specifically states: 'As the time drew near when Jesus would be taken up to heaven, he made up his mind and set out on his way to Jerusalem' (9:51). Ascension would follow death and resurrection.

John's teaching

John's great word for what happened at the Ascension is 'glorification'. Death by crucifixion, resurrection by the mighty power of God and ascension into heaven were the three stages of the glorification. In his prayer in John 17 Jesus prayed 'Father, the hour has come. Give glory to your Son, so that the Son may give glory to you' (17:1, see also 12:23, 13:31, 17:5). In the Ascension Jesus claimed to be 'going to the Father' (14:12, 28 and 16:28). Having reached the Father, Jesus 'will ask the Father and he will give you [disciples] another Helper, who will stay with you forever' (14:16); this 'Helper...who reveals the truth about God' will also speak about the exalted Jesus (15:26). Another aspect of the arrival in heaven will be to prepare a place for his disciples. Jesus said, 'There are many rooms in my Father's house, and I am going to prepare a place for you' (14:2).

Thus for the sake of the glorified Messiah the Father sends from heaven the Advocate, the Paraclete, and Helper, the Holy Spirit who takes the place of Jesus in the Church. Meanwhile Jesus, the Advocate on high, prepares places in heaven for those who believe in his name.

In the Revelation of John the ascended, ruling Christ is a major theme. Jesus is the child, born to the mysterious woman, who 'will rule over all nations' and is snatched away and taken to God and his throne (12:5). Jesus, the exalted Christ, told the lukewarm church of Laodicea that 'To those who win the victory I will give the right to sit beside me on my throne, just as I have been victorious and now sit by my Father on his throne' (3:21). Through his descent he had conquered the enemies of God and possessed the keys of death, Hades (1:18). John heard a loud voice in heaven saying, 'Now God's salvation has come! ... Now his Messiah has shown his authority! For the one [Satan] who stood before our God and accused our brothers day and night has been thrown out of heaven' (12:10). So as the triumphant and enthroned Messiah Jesus is 'the ruler of the kings of the world' (1:5) he will overcome all who rise against him for he is 'Lord of lords and King of kings' (17:14). Thus the heavenly chorus ascribes to him 'praise and honour, glory and might, for ever and ever' (5:13).

Paul's teaching

Already it has become clear through the study of the word *kyrios* that one great theme of Paul's teaching is that at his ascension Jesus was given the title of *Kyrios*. As a reward for his great condescension in becoming not merely a man but a servant of men, as well as entering into the abyss (Hades) which is the domain of Satan, God the Father raised him from the dead and exalted him so that he became Lord of the universe (Phil. 2:9–11). Thus, when he preached, Paul's message was that the Jesus who suffered and died is now Lord (2 Cor. 4:5), and he was proud to classify himself as a slave of this Lord Jesus Christ (Rom. 1:1; Gal. 1:10; Phil. 1:1). Obviously he believed that the exaltation of Jesus as Lord was a necessary preliminary before the Spirit could be given to the Church, for he claimed that no one can confess that 'Jesus is Lord' unless 'he is guided by the Holy Spirit' (1 Cor. 12:3) and many were truly confessing through his ministry that Jesus is Lord. As the converts left behind their commitment to Greek or Roman deities, to the worship of the Emperor or to the pursuit of selfish ends, they confessed in baptism that 'Jesus is Lord' and 'believed that God raised him from death' (Rom. 10:9).

Lying beneath the surface of Paul's writings is the further idea of the rule of Jesus as the Messiah King at the right hand of the Father. 'For Christ must rule until God defeats all enemies and puts them under his feet' (1 Cor. 15:25, see also Phil. 3:21b). As in the Book of Revelation, Jesus the exalted Lord Christ, views his enemies from his royal throne: Paul knows that the end of the age will only have come when 'Christ will overcome all spiritual rulers, authorities, and powers, and will hand over the Kingdom to God the Father' (1 Cor. 15:24).

For Paul the Ascension into heaven was the last of four stages in the work of redemption; it followed substitutionary death, descent into Hades and Resurrection from death and Hades. In these he was victorious as the Servant of God and as the Representative of men over sin, death, hell and Satan (Rom. 10:7, 14:9; Col. 1:18, 2:15). He has therefore become 'supreme over every spiritual ruler and authority' (Col. 2:10) and before him all creatures will one day fall upon their knees (Phil. 2:10).

In the Epistle to the Ephesians Paul developed the idea of the supremacy of Christ with special reference to his being 'to the church as supreme Lord over all things'. In other words 'God put all things under Christ's feet' so that, as the sovereign Lord, he can direct the life and history of the Church to the end planned by the Father (1:22). This means that Christians can face all the challenges in terms of trials, temptations and tribulations that the devil puts before them; they can wrestle successfully against the 'wicked spiritual forces in the heavenly world, the rulers, authorities, and cosmic powers of this dark age' (6:12) for the simple reason that God seated Christ 'at his right side in the heavenly world. Christ rules there above all heavenly rulers, authorities, powers, and lords' (1:20–21). The evil, satanic, powers which still cause sin and havoc in the world have only a limited existence; by his death, resurrection and ascension Christ gained victory over them and they will be completely vanquished at the end of the age. In a war the decisive battle may have already occurred at an early stage, but the war continues. The decisiveness of the battle is not recognised by all but it still means that victory is assured in the end. Only after the day of victory will the importance of the specific battle be recognised by all.

Paul sees Christian believers as united with Christ not only in death and resurrection (Rom. 6:1–13) but also in ascension. He told the Ephesian church, 'I ask that your minds may be opened to see his light, so that you will know what is the hope to which he has called you, how rich are the wonderful blessings he promises to his people, and how very great is his power at work in us who believe. This power working in us is the same as the mighty strength which he used when he raised Christ from death and seated him at his right side in the heavenly world' (Eph. 1:18–20). He went on to state that 'in our union with Christ Jesus he raised us up with him to rule with him in the heavenly world' (2:6). So their citizenship is in heaven, their true home (Col. 3:1–4).

The teaching of the Epistle to the Hebrews

Jesus as a human being had a status inferior to that of angels 'but we do see Jesus, who for a little while was made lower than the angels ... now crowned with glory and honour because of the death he suffered' (Heb. 2:9). The earthly life ended in the death on the cross but 'after achieving forgiveness for the sins of mankind, he sat down in heaven at the right-hand side of God, the Supreme Power' (1:3). As was noted in chapter three use is made of Psalm 110. Referring to Jesus he wrote 'God never said to any of his angels: "Sit here on my right until I put your enemies as a footstool under your feet"' (1:13, quoting Ps. 110:1). For the same purpose Psalm 45, another coronation psalm, was quoted: 'About the Son, however, God said: "Your kingdom, O God, will last for ever and ever! You rule over your people with justice. You love what is right and hate what is wrong. That is why God, your God, has chosen you and has given you the joy of an honour far greater than he gave to your companions"' (1:8–9; Ps. 45:6).

It is, however, in his further use of Psalm 110 verse 4, 'You will be a priest for ever, in the line of succession to Melchizedek', that he develops his own unique theme. Through human sufferings Jesus learned and achieved perfection, that is a total dedication to God (2:10, 5:9–10, 7:28). While the priestly descendants of Aaron sinned and died Jesus lives for ever and does not pass on his priesthood to another (7:23, 26). But if he is not an

Aaronic priest then he is of another line, the line of Melchizedek. This priest, who appears in and disappears from the story of Abraham in Genesis chapter 14 verses 17–20, was superior to both Abraham and Aaron for to him Abraham (from whom Aaron was to descend) gave tithes, which in the times of the patriarchs meant that he was giving to a person of higher station. Christ is a High Priest after the order of Melchizedek and thus his office as High Priest and his work as High Priest are superior to that of the Aaronic priesthood (Heb. 5:6, 10, 6:20, 7:1–7).

Also at one and the same time Jesus is High Priest and Sacrifice offered. He put away sins (9:26); he tasted death for every man (2:9) and by the shedding of his blood he gained for his followers forgiveness of sins (9:22). Using symbolic language drawn from the ritual of the Temple in the Old Testament, we say that he passed through the heavens (4:14), entered into the holy place of the heavenly Temple, taking with him his blood that had been shed on the Cross (9:12, 23–4). So the One who makes atonement is the same One who is the heavenly Mediator. As the Mediator in God's holy presence 'he is able, now and always, to save those who come to God through him, because he lives for ever to plead with God for them' (7:25). So Christians have a new and living way opened up for them to God and are therefore more privileged than the saints of the old covenant (10:20). By virtue of his ascension he becomes the forerunner of those who are to follow him (6:20).

Therefore for the writer of this epistle the ascended Jesus is the vindicated Messiah-King (1:13), the High Priest who lives forever (7:23–6), the Son of God (1:8) and the Lord (2:3, 7:14). While angels worship him he both rules the world and effectively intercedes for his followers on earth who face temptation and tribulation.

The teaching of Peter

Peter's doctrine may be stated briefly. First of all the Ascension is the means by which God gave glory to Jesus: God 'raised him from death and gave him glory' (1 Pet. 1:21). It was also the occasion when he was enthroned as the Messiah-King: after his descent into Hades where he preached to the imprisoned spirits Jesus was raised from death and now 'has gone to heaven and is at the right-hand side of God, ruling over all angels and heavenly authorities and powers' (1 Pet. 3:22).

Summary of the New Testament teaching

It has been wisely said that it is of profound significance that the New Testament clearly distinguishes the resurrection from the ascension of Jesus. As the Risen One, Jesus becomes the 'first-born among many brethren, (Rom. 8:29 RSV) and his resurrection is the beginning or the guarantee of the general resurrection of the dead (1 Cor. 15). But as the Ascended One he becomes the Sovereign One; that is, he is not only Lord of death but also Lord of the universe. Bearing this in mind the doctrine of the Ascension may be summed up in the following headings.

1. The exalted Jesus was declared to be and was enthroned as the Messiah-King, the One promised and predicted by the prophets of the Old Testament.

2. Because he overcame death and Hades the exalted Jesus was declared to be and was enthroned as the Lord of the whole universe, the King of kings.

3. As the Perfect, Obedient Man Jesus was rewarded by the Ascension and, at the same time, as the Son of God, he ascended into heaven by natural right.

4. The presence of the exalted Jesus in heaven means that there is truly Gospel, Good News, of forgiveness of sins in his name and reconciliation to God to be preached.

5. The exalted Jesus becomes the Head of the Church which is his body on earth.

6. The fullness of the Spirit for the Church is given because Jesus is glorified. The Father and the Son send the Spirit into the world and the Son gives spiritual gifts to his Church to work in his name and power.

7. In heaven Jesus, the Lord, prepares a place for those who believe on his name for where he is those who are united to him in faith will also be.

8. In heaven, Jesus the Priest-King, prays for his people as they struggle on earth against sin and tribulation.

Whether all these doctrines or principles can be fitted together into a coherent doctrine is questionable. As our subject relates to the heavenly scene and also concerns both exalted humanity and eternal deity in glory this should not worry us.

However, from these doctrines and heavenly realities the writers in the New Testament draw various practical applications. For example Paul told the Colossian church: 'You have been raised to life with Christ, so set your hearts on the things that are in heaven, where Christ sits on his throne at the right-hand side of God. Keep your minds fixed on things there, not on things here on earth. For you have died and your life is hidden with Christ in God' (Col. 3:1). And the writer to the

Hebrew Christians claimed that 'to have faith is to be sure of the things we hope for, to be certain of the things we cannot see' (Heb. 11:1), of which the ascended Jesus is an important part.

A PRAYER (FROM THE BOOK OF COMMON PRAYER)
Grant, we beseech thee, almighty God, that like as we do believe thy only-begotten Son our Lord Jesus Christ to have ascended into the heavens; so we may also in heart and mind thither ascend, and with him continually dwell, who liveth and reigneth with thee and the Holy Ghost, one God, world without end. Amen.

There are not many books dealing with the Ascension: see, however, H. B. Swete, *The Ascended Christ* (1910) and J. G. Davies, *He Ascended into Heaven* (1958).

5 Jesus, Lord of the nations

MANY PEOPLE FIND it very difficult to grasp the general principles of the teaching in the New Testament concerning the kingdom of God, a subject which was often on the lips of Jesus. The reason for the problem is that the kingdom has both a present and a future reality. The reign of God over the universe, in the sense that all creatures live in obedience to the laws of God and there is no evil in nature or society, will come into being only at the end of this age, that is at the end of time as we know it. This is that future of which Paul speaks when he says that 'God will rule completely over all' (1 Cor. 15:28b) and is that of which various psalmists and prophets in the Old Covenant spoke. Psalm 22:27 reads 'All nations will remember the Lord. From every part of the world they will turn to him; all races will worship him. The Lord is king, and he rules the nations' (see also Ps. 145 and Dan. 7:13-14).

But if God is truly God now, he must also rule over the world at the present time even though a majority of his subjects is ignorant of his rule or refuses to acknowledge it. We believe that God rules over the seasons of the year and over the world of nature (Matt. 6:25-30). We believe that he rules over nations and their history even though we are aware that these nations do not actually obey his laws. In saying this we mean that the power that rulers have is a delegated power and that they only function within the limits which God allows to them within the execution of what we call divine providence (Ps. 75:7; Jer. 27:5; Dan. 4:3; Rom. 13:1-5). The end to which human history is moving is actually God's appointed end. Then also, we believe that God's rule is (or should be) explicit within the hearts of those who are submitted to his rule; again, in Paul's words, the kingdom of God in his Church is 'righteousness, peace, and joy which the Holy Spirit gives' (Rom. 14:17).

It is the specific teaching of Paul and John that the invisible reign of God in this age has been delegated, since the Ascension, to the exalted Jesus, now Messiah and Lord. In this chapter we shall discuss the rule of Christ over nations and human history while in the next we shall look at the relationship of this Lordship to his rule in the Church. It will be seen that his reign over the Church is a reign of grace but his reign over Satanic forces in the world is one of judgment.

Paul's teaching

It will be useful, first of all, to look at one central Pauline passage:

> Christ will overcome all spiritual rulers, authorities, and powers, and will hand over the Kingdom to God the Father. For Christ must rule until God defeats all enemies and puts them under his feet. The last enemy to be defeated will be death. . . . For the scripture says, 'God put *all* things under his feet.' It is clear, of course, that the words 'all things' do not include God himself, who puts all things under Christ. But when all things have been placed under Christ's rule, then he himself, the Son, will place himself under God, who placed all things under him; and God will rule completely over all (1 Cor. 15:24–8).

The context of this passage is the discussion by Paul of the resurrection of Christ and of Christians. The resurrection of the believers is dependent on that of Christ and will take place at the second coming of Christ. Behind the whole passage lies a development of thought from Psalm 110:1 and Psalm 8:6 (which is quoted).

The rule of Jesus, the Christ, began at his exaltation as we have already seen from other Pauline passages, Philippians chapter 2 verses 6–11 for example. It extends to his second coming. By his exaltation he triumphed over death and Satanic powers but although he personally overcame these evil forces they remain in the universe and are still at work in human history (as the existence of war, crime, and disease abundantly shows). While he has demonstrated and proved that he is stronger than Satan and is the Victor over the powers of death, he has not yet openly and finally destroyed these forces which are hostile to the rule of God. He allows them to function in a limited way in the world in order that, in the difficulties and problems they cause, human beings can see the great value of the gospel and the grace and salvation which it offers. (In other parts of the New Testament (Col. 2:15; 2 Tim. 1:10; 1 Pet. 3:22) the evil forces and death itself are viewed as already overcome and even abolished. The reason for this is that the death, resurrection and ascension of Jesus constitute the decisive battle in the great spiritual war that will end victoriously with the resurrection of Christ's disciples.)

In 2 Thessalonians 2:3–10 Paul teaches that before the final victory of Christ 'the wicked one' (or 'the man of sin') will appear and claim to be divine and thus to be worshipped. He is some kind of antichrist and scholars are not in agreement as to his identity. However, he will come 'with the power of Satan and perform all kinds of false miracles and wonders' in order to deceive people but 'when the Lord Jesus comes, he will kill him with the breath from his mouth and destroy him with his dazzling presence'. Along with his master, Satan, he will ultimately perish.

At his second coming Christ will be shown to have defeated death because there will be the resurrection of the dead. This universal event will be the sign that the evil powers in the world have now been fully and finally vanquished. His saving work in history, begun in his incarnation, will then be fulfilled. He will have completely overcome the evil brought into the world by Adam (Rom. 5:12). So he will hand over to the Father a redeemed humanity and a universe, restored to a proper creaturely submissiveness. Then God 'will rule completely over all' when a completely new order of everlasting reality will be brought into being.

This kingdom of Christ, stretching from his ascension to second coming is sometimes called his mediatorial kingdom, for in this period he not only rules over the world as king but he is the One through whom human beings are reconciled to God. At one and the same time the Ruler is also the Saviour and Mediator (1 Tim. 2:5). So it is not surprising that Paul states that God 'rescued us from the power of darkness and brought us safe into the kingdom of his dear Son, by whom we are set free' (Col. 1:13–14). Here Paul states that Christians have a share in the kingdom of Christ. But what does he mean? Is he thinking of the Church in which is the rule of Christ and in which rule Christians share? Probably not. Rather he is developing a related but different line of thought. His reference to the kingdom in verse 13 has to be connected with his statement in verse 12 that 'God has reserved for his people in the kingdom of light' an inheritance. Paul is teaching that in union with Christ the believer is exalted into heaven, the kingdom of light, and is seated with the heavenly company which delights in the glory of God. It is to be remembered that the kingdom of Christ is a more comprehensive term than the word 'Church'. In Colossians 1:13–14 (as in Eph. 2:6) the kingdom is the universal sphere of power and glory of the exalted Christ who has rescued Christians from the sphere of the influence of the powers of darkness and made them to share in his glory.

So, for Paul, Christ is ruling now, but secretly, waiting for the moment when his rule will be open, universal and complete.

The teaching of John, the 'Seer'

The theme of the last book of the Bible is the victory of the exalted Christ and of his Church over the dragon (Satan) and his accomplices (earthly and heavenly). It was written at a time when Christians were being persecuted and churches being driven underground because they would not submit to the demands by the Roman State that the Emperor be worshipped as 'Lord and God'. To John on Patmos, himself a victim of the persecution, God granted visions of the certain triumph of Christ and his followers. By these the Christians were taught that events were not what they appeared to be. Thus the beast that comes out of the abyss to persecute and kill the Christians appears to be victorious, and indeed, as far as human history narrowly conceived is concerned, is victorious. But the merriment of the world in its triumph will be only temporary for, as Revelation chapter 11 verses 15–19 puts it, God will intervene:

> Then the seventh angel blew his trumpet, and there were loud voices in heaven, saying, 'The power to rule over the world belongs now to our Lord and his Messiah, and he will rule for ever and ever!' Then the twenty-four elders who sit on their thrones in front of God threw themselves face downwards and worshipped God, saying:
> 'Lord God Almighty, who is and who was!
> We thank you that you have taken your great power and have begun to rule!
> The heathen were filled with rage, because the time for your anger has come, the time for the dead to be judged.
> The time has come to reward your servants the prophets, and all your people, all who worship you, great and small alike.
> The time has come to destroy those who destroy the earth!'

This passage reminds us of what Paul wrote in 1 Corinthians chapter 15 verses 24–28. Christ will finally conquer all his foes and then God will rule over a perfect, renewed creation.

Throughout Revelation Jesus Christ is pictured as the mighty Victor and the great Conqueror. His vanquished foes are death, Hades (the abyss), the dragon (Satan), the beast (Roman Empire and emperors), the false prophet (the organisation behind the cult of emperor worship) and the people who actually worship the beast. Jesus tells the persecuted churches, 'I am the first and the last. I am the living one! I was dead, but now I am alive for ever and ever. I have authority over death and the world of the dead' (1:17–18). Therefore he is as a conqueror, riding to conquer (6:2). With the help of his heavenly host he defeated Satan and his angels and cast them down from heaven (at his exaltation) so that the heavenly voice could proclaim: 'Now God's salvation has come! Now God has shown his power as King! Now his Messiah has shown his authority! For the one who stood before our God and accused our brothers day and night has been thrown out of heaven' (12:10). So the truth of history, even though the Roman rulers and men since their day cannot see it, is summarised in the heavenly song, 'Lord God Almighty, how great and wonderful are your deeds! King of the nations, how right and true are your ways!' (15:3).

But Satan is still free to roam the earth. Yet when the nations gather together under Antichrist (cf. 2 Thess. 2) at the end of the age to oppose the will of God and the Saviour of the world, Jesus Christ, they will miserably fail. 'They will fight against the Lamb; but the Lamb, together with his called, chosen and faithful followers, will defeat them, because he is Lord of lords and King of kings' (Rev. 17:14). For Paul the Christians are united to Christ in his exaltation in heaven (Eph. 1:3–4) but for John they share in his triumph over his foes. These are two ways of saying basically the same thing. In Paul the victorious rule of Jesus, the Lord, is primarily associated with the defeat of the cosmic, evil powers, whereas for John Jesus is the King of the earthly kings. Yet since the latter are in the employment of Satan the two writers are really proclaiming the same positive theme, one writing before, and one writing in, the persecution of the churches by the Roman Empire. John ends his visions with one of the New Jerusalem, the new order which will come into being after the destruction of all evil, and in the centre of this new heaven and earth he sees 'the throne of God and of the Lamb' which is the same as saying, with Paul, that God will be 'all in all'. God's will is sure ultimately to triumph.

One important dimension of the new Jerusalem is the 'marriage of the Lamb'. When the war is over and won, a feast of joy is celebrated and 'happy are those who have been invited to the wedding-feast of the Lamb' (19:9). This bringing home of the bride, her reception into the perfect kingdom of God, the heavenly Jerusalem, is the final work of Christ the King. The community on earth joins the community in heaven. Here, of course John is developing Old Testament themes (Jer. 2:2, 3:1–3; Ezek. 16:7; Is. 54:6–8, 62:4) and providing similar teaching to Paul (2 Cor. 11:2; Eph. 5:22–3).

There remains the problem of the kingdom of a thousand years (20:1–6). This has been interpreted in a variety of ways: for example, as the period between the exaltation and second coming of Christ (Augustine, *City of God* 20:7); as the period from the collapse of the Roman Empire to the second coming of Christ (Jerusalem Bible); as a literal reign of Christ and his saints/martyrs on earth for one thousand years immediately before the final battle with Gog and Magog and the general resurrection of the dead (Scofield Reference Bible), or of a period of revival of Christianity at the end of this age before the second coming of Christ (Geneva Bible, later editions). It is neither appropriate nor possible to discuss the pros and cons here. Whatever interpretation we give we merely strengthen the general theme which we gain from the rest of the book that Jesus

Christ rules as King and Lord over the nations of the world.

Christ the Lord today

In England today the people know that the monarch reigns because her presence is seen in Parliament on ceremonial occasions, her portrait appears on the currency and on postage stamps, and from time to time the national anthem is sung on public occasions beginning with the words 'God save our gracious Queen'. But the rule of Christ as Lord of the nations cannot be demonstrated in the same way. One is not able to point to specific events or objects which prove to people of a reasonable disposition that Christ rules the world. Indeed, the wars which have occurred between nations, the natural disasters which have befallen the world, and the seemingly impossibly complex maze of events in human history have sometimes led sincere people to doubt the existence of God, let alone his rule in human history.

The doctrine that Christ is Lord of the nations and of human history is only meaningful through the eyes of faith. It is only because the Christian believes that God was truly in Jesus of Nazareth reconciling the world to himself that he can begin to believe that this same God-Man is in control of human destiny. Further, it is only because he believes that the apostles were directly guided in their creation and development of Christian teaching that he can take the writings of Paul and John seriously when they write of the Lordship of Christ in history.

Often zealous Christians have tried to see within European and Middle-Eastern history specific evidence for the Lordship of Christ. In the nineteenth century when Napolean advanced on Rome many Protestants believed that the Lord Christ was governing and guiding history towards the fulfilment of what they believed was his will, but which was, in fact, their own interpretation of Revelation 18. They believed that the taking of Rome was the beginning of events leading towards the destruction of the Papacy, the Second Coming and a possible millennial reign of Christ. A decade later they knew that their interpretation was merely speculation! In recent times the most common example of this same habit of mind has been the zeal of many, especially North American evangelicals, to see in the geographical expansion of the nation-state of Israel the fulfilment of what they say is God's will revealed in Scripture but which, in all honesty, is more correctly described as their interpretation of prophecy. This type of thinking which sees the Lord Christ working for the Israelis and against the Arabs is speculation, as was the earlier thinking concerning the role of Napoleon in the purposes of God. Only Christ, the heavenly Ruler, knows what he is doing when he is guiding the history of individual nations and tribes. What glimpses we have in Scripture into the mystery of his rule are notoriously difficult to interpret and the massive number of mistakes made by our forefathers in this field of eschatological speculation should lead us to be cautious. Only by faith, on the basis of the historical Incarnation, do we confess the rule of Christ now and look for his coming rule when all will confess that he is Lord.

This tendency to what may be termed overassurance in interpreting history is found in its most popular form in that interpretation known as dispensationalism, traditionally associated with the Plymouth Brother J. N. Darby, Dallas, Theological Seminary, and the Scofield Reference Bible. Recently Hal Lindsey, a popular advocate of this school of thought, has attempted, in his best-selling *The Late Great Planet Earth*, to see clearly and unmistakably the meaning of current events in the Near East in terms of God's purposes and Christ's rule. Regrettably also, even in the writings of a justly praised historian like the late K. S. Latourette, author of many fine books, there is at times a display of supreme confidence in his own ability to claim to be able to trace with accuracy the results within the complexities of human history of the operation of the grace of Christ.

Whether or not there is a genuinely Christian approach to the writing of history is a difficult question to answer and no doubt it will be discussed by scholars for years to come.[1] Happily both Christian historians and Christian non-historians can take comfort from the general doctrine that God through Christ is in charge of his world and its history and will bring it to his own conclusion and vindicate his people.

But what are we to make of Paul's talk of 'principalities and powers'? The apostle presupposed that before the Incarnation the world (presumably from Adam's sinful act, itself related to a rebellion amongst the spiritual servants of God) was in some kind of bondage to invisible evil powers which governed the sphere which exists between God and man. By his resurrection and ascension Jesus Christ cut his way through these powers and broke their grip on the world. He therefore triumphed over them in that he marched through them to his rightful place with God. They could not prevent his triumphal procession.

Today even the most conservatively biblical of us find these statements to be somewhat mythological. We find it difficult, against the background of modern science, to picture a band of evil angels guarding the spiritual route from men to God and directing the destinies of men on earth. However, many of us do not find it difficult to believe that in our universe, certainly upon our earth, there are definite evil forces at work which at times appear to grip individuals (e.g. tyrants and dictators) and groups of people (e.g. extreme organisations which plot to destroy and kill) and create an evil ethos or hateful feeling within a nation (e.g. that the killing of millions of human beings by the Hitler régime was somehow acceptable).

Paul's message for modern times is that Jesus Christ, by his victory over death in his bodily resurrection, and by his direct entry into the spiritual world where God is alone supreme, has triumphed over all the forces in our universe which drag mankind down into decadence and which keep people from loving God. Jesus, the God-Man, is now at the centre of that spiritual world upon which our earthly world is dependent and we believe that he will return to this earthly sphere in order to destroy once and forever these evil forces of which already he has shown himself to be the master.

Lord of structures?

An important insight claimed by exponents of Liberation Theology (e.g. G. Gutierrez, *A Theology of Liberation*) is that sin is found in social and political structures in human society as well as in individual hearts. Thus to preach only the need for individual conversion does not necessarily guarantee improvement in a society in terms of social righteousness for if the structures are sinful then they actually propagate sin. For structures to be sinful means that they aid or cause injustice; liberated structures should produce justice, mercy and righteousness. Not all Christians take this point and partly because of this, and probably more because of its use of the Bible, liberation theology gets a bad press in conservative circles.[2]

There is continuing disagreement among evangelical Christians as to whether it can be affirmed, let alone proclaimed, that the Lordship of Christ relates now, in this age of sinfulness, to the structures of human society. Another way of posing the question is to ask whether in this age the kingdom of God (kingdom of Christ) relates directly or indirectly to the way in which we organise our national life in its many aspects. All agree that Christ rules over the nations in the general sense outlined above and all agree that Christ should be seen to be ruling in his churches. So we ask, is there any basis in the New Testament for claiming that the structures and spheres of human society (including education, organised labour etc.) should be directly subject to the rule of the law of Christ, according to his revealed will as found in Scripture? There are three passages from Paul that we must briefly examine. They may help us to understand the request 'may your kingdom come' (Matt. 6:10) in the Lord's Prayer.

First is 1 Corinthians chapter 11 verse 3 where Paul wrote, 'I want you to understand that Christ is supreme over every man, the husband is supreme over his wife, and God is supreme over Christ'. Here we have an hierarchy of God, Christ, man, wife. A problem of meaning here is whether the men over whom Christ rules are only the 'men in Christ', the new humanity, or the whole human race, every man of the old Adamic race. This seems to be settled if we understand the Greek (*kephalē*) used here and translated 'supreme over' by the Good News Bible to mean not only head or ruler but also 'source of ' or 'origin of'. Christ is the source of all men since he is the agent of creation (1 Cor. 8:6).[3] If he is the source of all things he has a natural right to be the active ruler over all things. Therefore it appears his law should be the basis for the organisation of different groupings, from the family through to the government, within the nation.

Secondly, there is Ephesians 5:21–6:9. Here there is a clear statement, closely integrated with the rule of Christ over his Church, that wives are to obey husbands, husbands are to love their wives, children are to obey parents, parents are to educate their children, slaves are to be obedient to masters, masters are to treat their slaves respectfully. If Paul's teaching has reference to both the Church and the whole humanity of which Christ, the Head, is the 'source' then, in today's terms, Paul is saying that Christ's law should rule not only families but also educational institutions, governments, labour organisations, employers' organisations and the like.

Thirdly, there is Romans 13 where Paul teaches that the human rulers of men have been placed in their position by God and thus are to be obeyed as God's servants. Further, human relationships in society are to be governed by the law of love, love for the neighbour. Now the word which is translated in verse 1 as 'authorities' can mean either a human government or an angelic power which, in God's ordering of the world, stands behind each of the major powers on earth. Jews believed that God ruled the world through a hierarchy of angels who superintended, on his behalf, the human rulers on earth. But we have already noticed that Christ is portrayed by Paul as the conqueror of principalities and powers, the ruler of angels and men. Thus Christ may be said to be ruling over the governments of the nations and it may be said of them that they have a duty to rule the citizens according to the law of Christ.

There is also a passage in 1 Peter which is worth quoting in full:

> For the sake of the Lord submit to every human authority: to the Emperor, who is the supreme authority, and to the governors, who have been appointed by him to punish the evildoer and to praise those who do good. For God wants you to silence the ignorant talk of foolish people by the good things you do. Live as free people; do not, however, use your freedom to cover up any evil, but live as God's slaves. Respect everyone, love your fellow-believers, fear God, and respect the Emperor (1 Pet. 2: 13–17).

This passage is similar to Romans 13. It is here implied that human governments are there, in God's rule over and in his world, in order not only to protect the physical well-being of the citizens but also to promote their moral welfare. They have been appointed in God's providence to 'praise those who do good'. This provokes the thought that it is only as they set for themselves righteous standards and just ends that human rulers can in fact promote moral goodness. So the question arises, 'Will they not set the correct standards to the degree in which they are subject to the rule of Christ the Lord?'

If we conclude that the general teaching of the New Testament is that the rule of Christ should begin to operate now within human society and its structures of government, then we have much more thinking to do concerning exactly what we mean when we talk of the rule of Christ. Is it only the contents of the ten commandments or is it more? Is the rule of Christ in society a message that the Church should proclaim to the world along with, or after, it has preached the gospel?[4]

A PRAYER

O God our Father we are sometimes overwhelmed by the compexities of our modern world and by our inability to understand the events which make up international relations. We see atheism triumphing in one part of the world, communities attacking each other in another part and abject poverty in yet another part. In this situation we are so glad to know that your Son, our Saviour, the Lord Jesus, knows all that we know and much more besides, and that he will, in your good time, bring human history to the goal which you have set for it. Grant to us, we pray, such a trust in you and your word that we shall live in this world as true citizens of both this world and the world to come, for the sake of the same Jesus Christ. Amen.

NOTES
[1] In the meantime, however, *A Christian View of History*? (ed. G. Marsden and F. Roberts, 1976) is helpful reading.
[2] For an introduction to liberation theology see the booklet by E. Gibbs, *World Upside Down* (1976).
[3] See further F. F. Bruce, *1 and 2 Corinthians* (1971), p. 103.
[4] For stimulating reading see the booklet by C. Sugden, *Social Gospel or No Gospel?* (1974).

6 Jesus, Lord of the Church

IF THE EXALTED Jesus is the unseen Lord of nations then he is certainly also the Lord of the Church. Paul's favourite term for the Church was apparently 'the body of Christ' of which, he teaches in Ephesians and Colossians, the exalted Jesus is the Head (Greek, *kephalē*). Before looking at the appropriate passages it will be helpful to remind ourselves of the way in which evangelical Protestants have interpreted the expression 'body of Christ' so that we can check our traditional understanding in this sensitive area with the actual teaching of Paul.

Protestants have generally taken 'body of Christ' to be the biblical term which is equivalent in theological discourse to 'the invisible Church' or 'the mystical body of Christ'. By these terms is usually meant the total company of true Christians of all times and of all places on earth and in heaven (and, sometimes, yet to be born). For example the influential Presbyterian Westminster Confession of Faith (1648) states in chapter xxv: 'The catholic or universal Church, which is invisible, consists of the whole number of the elect, that have been, are, or shall be gathered into one, under Christ the Head thereof; and is the spouse, the body, the fulness of him that filleth all in all.' The Holy Spirit is said to regenerate or to create a new nature within each Christian believer (John 3:1-8) and by this spiritual link the believer is joined to Christ (and God) and to other similar regenerate believers. Only God knows who are the true Christians and where, therefore, is the invisible Church (invisible, that is, to men but visible to God who is Spirit). Just as we often think of the human body as having within it an invisible human spirit (i.e. soul or mind) so the thought is of the body of Christ as the total number of people in whom is the one Spirit, the Spirit of God.

This particular understanding was begun by the Reformers in the sixteenth century as they learned from Augustine of Hippo, and was developed by Protestants in later generations as they engaged in controversy with Roman Catholics. In more recent times the idea of the invisible Church has been used for purposes which would probably have shocked theologians of earlier centuries. It has been used to justify the splitting of supposed luke-warm or doctrinally impure denominations, of the creation of many new missionary and philanthropic societies, the regarding of visible unity among Christians as unimportant, and the heightening of the understanding of Christianity as basically and primarily an individualistic relationship with God in Christ.

As a corollary of the doctrine of the Church as invisible the local church which is obviously visible is seen from this viewpoint as a mixed company of the regenerate and unregenerate, the true and the false believer. The true believer is seen as united to God and to others, both in that congregation and in others, by the Spirit, but only related to other unregenerate members of the local congregation as he is related to other people in any human community, by common interests and activities. The local visible church, as such, has no direct relation to the body of Christ and cannot be called the body of Christ. The relation which the local church has is with other local churches to which it is joined in a denominational or parochial framework.

What has just been stated about the local congregation is traditional Protestant teaching. However recently, through the influence of the charismatic movement,[1] which has affected virtually all denominations in Europe and North America, there has grown up the custom of calling the local fellowship of Christians by the term 'body of Christ' and of referring to 'body-fellowship' and 'body-life' when speaking of the mutual relations and activities of the local church. Sometimes this usage appears to be neither metaphorical nor analogical but approaches the literal; sometimes it appears to be informed by careful study of Paul's theology and at other times to be merely repeated as the latest kind of 'in' language.

Paul's teaching in 1 Corinthians and Romans

If we read Romans 12 and 1 Corinthians 12 we find that Paul appeals to the analogy of the human body, which has many individual parts all made and needing to work together, for the proper functioning of the body, in order to impress upon the members of the churches in Rome and Corinth that individual Christians, since they belong to Christ, also belong to each other and therefore should function harmoniously together in the local situation, as do the parts of the human body in the one body. In Romans 12 Paul calls the church to holy and humble living and then proceeds to tell the members that each one has a gift with a function and that he or she should use this for the good of others and for the glory of God. The context in 1 Corinthians 12 is the use and abuse of spiritual gifts within the local church. Paul teaches that there is one Lord of the whole Church, Jesus Christ, and one Spirit, who brings the spiritual life and gifts of Christ to the people of God. The church in Corinth is then compared to the human body with each member having a gift and function so that 'if one member suffers all the other members suffer and if one member is praised all the other members share his happiness'. In verses 27–30 Paul appears to use the idea of the Church as the body of Christ in a larger context than the local church. All the churches founded by the apostles can also be thought of as Christ's body for they are all linked to him.

Scholars have pointed out that to call a specific community a 'body' is not uncommon in Greek literature. However, because this usage existed, we cannot automatically assume that Paul's meaning is totally conditioned by contemporary usage in the language in which he preached. That is to say, it cannot be taken for granted that the two words 'of Christ' are merely a qualifying genitive, meaning 'belonging to Christ'. Rather it is better to see behind the term 'body of Christ' Paul's familiar teaching of 'the many' (Rom. 5:15–21, cf. Isaiah 53:11) being 'in Christ' (Rom. 12:5; Gal. 3:28). He held that Christ was crucified for his *people* (1 Cor. 1:13); that God made Christ to be sin *for us* (2 Cor. 5:21); that Christ became a curse *for us* and gave himself *for us* (Gal. 1:4; 1 Tim. 2:6; Rom. 5:6). Those sinners who believe in him become this people, 'the many', and are spoken of as being crucified, dead, buried and raised with Christ (Rom. 6:3ff; Gal. 2:19; Col. 2:12–13, 20, 3:1,9).

Paul contrasts the people 'in Adam' with the people 'in Christ' (1 Cor. 15:22; Rom. 5:12ff). Adam and Christ are made, as it were, to stand over against each other as the two great figures at the beginning of two worlds, two creations, two humanities, one old age and one new age. In their actions and fate are the actions of all who belong to them and who are 'in them'. All human beings are 'in Adam' sharing in his sin and death; all who believe the gospel are 'in Christ' sharing in his triumph over sin and death.

So we can see that the logic of Paul's thinking requires that a person is united to Christ in his confession of faith (with which baptism is associated—see 1 Cor. 6:11; Eph. 5:26) and in being so united also becomes a member of the body of Christ and is made by Christ to drink of the one Spirit (1 Cor. 12:13). Experientially, it is probably the case that union with Christ, incorporation into his body, and receiving his Spirit are contemporaneous but in Paul's theological logic the order is Christ → body of Christ → Spirit.

This all means that while Paul probably took from contemporary usage the term 'body' to describe the relationship of a specific group of people to each other (e.g. in a city-state) he did not make the unity and diversity of the group the primary thrust of his thought. Neither did he make the spiritual indwelling of the Spirit his first principle (which traditional evangelical thought has tended to do, as was pointed out above) for he is not thinking of a body as being of two parts, material (flesh and bone) and spiritual (soul). Rather, it is in virtue of the belonging to and inclusion in 'the many' for whom Christ died and rose that an individual believer becomes a member of the body of Christ. In being joined by faith to Christ and in union with Christ, he becomes, as it were, a toe or a rib in his body, the people of God which is manifested and functions in a specific time and place in human history. It is perhaps not necessary to point out that for Paul the idea of being a Christian and not being a member of a specific church was impossible.

Paul's teaching in Ephesians and Colossians

By the time these two letters were written the words 'body of Christ' had apparently achieved for Paul the status of a technical theological term. Not only is the Church called without explanation the 'body of Christ' (Eph. 1:23, 4:13) and Christian believers 'Christ's members' (Eph. 5:30) but 'body' as a description of the Church is used in an absolute sense (Col. 1:18, 24, 2:19, 3:15 and Eph. 4:4), that is without the genitive 'of Christ'. It is also to be noted that in Ephesians 3:6 the Gentiles are said to be (literally) 'fellow-body' (Greek *sun-sōma*), with the Jews.

The basic logic of Paul's teaching in these two epistles, both written from prison around AD 60, is basically that of Romans and 1 Corinthians. The Church is the body of Christ in that all believers, 'the many', were included in him, as the Second Adam, in his redeeming acts of death and resurrection. Also 'the many' included both Jews and Gentiles. 'For Christ himself has brought us peace by making Jews and Gentiles one people. With his own body he broke down the wall that separated them and kept them enemies' (Eph. 2:14). The body here is the physical body given in sacrifice upon the Cross but in verse 15 Paul speaks of Christ by his death creating 'one new people' and uniting both races into 'one body' (verse 16). That is the 'new man' who is 'in Christ' is not viewed by God as being Jew or Gentile but rather as a member of the new race, the new people of God, in which the old distinctions will have no meaning.

What is basically new in these two epistles is the teaching that Christ is the Head of this body. We read that God has put all things under the feet of Christ and 'has made him the head over all things for the church, which is his body' (Eph. 1:22-3 RSV). In the Good News Bible the 'head over all things' becomes, in a neat paraphrase, 'supreme Lord over all things'. As the Head he has at his disposal all the gifts needed by the Church. Again Paul wrote: 'So the one who came down is the same one who went up, above and beyond the heavens, to fill the whole universe with his presence. It was he who "gave gifts to mankind"; he appointed some to be apostles, others to be prophets, others to be evangelists, others to be pastors and teachers' (Eph. 4:10-11). The Church enjoys fellowship with him not on terms which apply between fellow members of the body but on terms appropriate to him as Head (Col. 1:18, 2:10, 19; Eph. 4:15-16). Christ is Head of the body not only by the donation of God the Father but also because he loved the Church and gave himself for her (Eph. 5:23-5).

What we now have to resolve can be put in the form of two questions. When Paul speaks of Christ the Head of the Church does he have in mind the analogy of the total human body (including the head) and thus does he see the Church as a decapitated body and Christ as the separated head which, by the operation of the Spirit, becomes united with the body? Or have we here not one but two analogies (that is the Church = Body of Christ and Christ = Head or Ruler) which are at times integrated?

In favour of the view that Paul is thinking of one body of which Christ is the head and Christians the rest of the body (from neck to toe) can be quoted such passages as:

We must grow up in every way to Christ who is the Head. Under his control all the different parts of the body fit together and the whole body is held together by every joint with which it is provided. So when each separate part works as it should, the whole body grows and builds itself up through love (Eph. 4:15-16).

... Christ, who is the head of the body. Under Christ's control the whole body is nourished and held together by its joints and ligaments, and it grows as God wants it to grow (Col. 2:19).

Against this view it must be reckoned first of all that Paul still speaks of the Church as the *whole* body (Eph. 4:16) and in 1 Corinthians 12:16 he uses the example of the eye as a part of the body thus showing that for him (at least in that context) the body was the *whole* body including the head. Then, secondly, from the viewpoint of physiology it is difficult, as much for a man of the first as of the twentieth century, to picture a body which is nourished from the head and growing up to the head. It is of importance to note that the Greek text has 'the head from *whom*' not 'the head from *which*' (Col. 2:19; Eph. 4:15-6), suggesting that for Paul 'head' and 'body' are not two parts of one whole but rather that 'head' is of a different order to 'body'. Thirdly, Christ as Head cannot meaningfully be thought of as part of his own body, the very body which is involved in the process of growth towards maturity and which must be already 'in Christ'. Fourthly, Paul also teaches that the husband is the head of the wife (Eph. 5:23) by which he does not mean that the physical head (eyes, ears etc.) of the married woman is in fact her husband. He means the husband is head in the sense that the wife is subject to him as he loves her. Fifthly, God is said by Paul to be the Head of Christ, while Christ is the Head of every man, and each husband is head of his wife (1 Cor. 11:3). Now to say that God is the Head of Christ is not to say that Christ is the body of God!

Taking these arguments into consideration it would appear that Paul's teaching about Christ as Head of all things and specifically Head of the Church is not, strictly speaking, a part of his teaching concerned the Church as the body of Christ, but is, rather, superimposed upon it. The Headship of Christ is similar in meaning to the Lordship of Christ; the exalted Jesus is Head of the Church in a similar way to that in which a man is said to be head of a state or of a school. Jesus Christ is Head of the Church in that he is its Ruler, the one with supreme authority.

Also, taking into account the Hebraic background and the Hebrew words for 'head' and 'beginning' which are closely related, we can say that Paul is teaching that Christ is the source (in the sense of the fount and beginning) of the spiritual life, ministry and gifts of the Church.[2]

The Church, visible or invisible

What can we say of the traditional evangelical understanding of the Church as (primarily and sometimes only) the 'mystical body of Christ' or 'the Church invisible'?

To be fair to our forefathers we must first affirm that there is truly a Church, the only Church, which is the mystical body of Christ. As God looks from heaven and takes all history and peoples into his gaze he sees the total number of believers, the 'many' for whom Christ died as the Second Adam, and he sees them as united to Christ, thus becoming his body. It is this company who will form the population of the new age which will follow the second coming of Christ and the judgment of the nations. Of this body Christ is both Saviour and Head. In Ephesians and Colossians it is this total number seen as one whole body that Paul often has in mind. For example when he speaks of Christ being made 'head of all things for the church, which is his body' it is this universal Church of which he writes. To be 'in Christ' is to be of the body of Christ and here there is 'neither Jew nor Greek, slave nor free, male nor female' for all are one in Christ (Gal. 3:28).

In today's scene, with all the competing denominations and groups that we have created in our management of the visible churches, it still remains true that to be united to Christ is to be everlastingly united to other believers in the body of Christ. From the divine perspective the Anglican, Methodist, Baptist and Lutheran all belong to one Church, the Church of which Jesus Christ is Head. It has been usual in Protestantism to equate the 'one, holy, catholic Church' of the Creed, with this invisible Church. This is perhaps legitimate although historically the expression did have a primary reference to the actual totality of visible churches in the world.

Having said this we must hasten to affirm also that the unity of which Paul speaks cannot be restricted to the invisible Church. It is, in fact, on the basis of being together in Christ that Paul deduces the necessity of a visible, outward manifestation of the body of Christ. In Corinth the congregation of Christians, called by Paul the body of Christ (1 Cor. 12:27), is censured by Paul because it is divided into groupings associated with different apostles—or even with Christ. He asked, 'Is Christ divided?' by which, in context, he is asking them to consider that the church should be one in both theory and reality. He certainly believed that the churches in Rome (Rom. 12:4–5) and Corinth (1 Cor. 12:12ff.) should function harmoniously within their own local situations as a human body in good health functions. And, even in the epistles where he dwells on the universal and everlasting nature of the Church, he still has time to impress upon the readers that the local church should truly be the body of Christ. He told the Christians of Ephesus, 'No more lying, then! Everyone must tell the truth to his fellow-believer, because we are all members together in the body of Christ' (Eph. 4:25). To the Colossian Christians he wrote: 'The peace that Christ gives is to guide you in the decisions you make; for it is to this peace that God has called you together in the one body' (Col. 3:15). Also it is worthy of note that Paul expected the local church to be an example of harmonious holiness for the world to see (1 Cor. 6:16, 10:16–22; 2 Cor. 6:14ff.). The local church is a microcosm of the total Church.

It is difficult to imagine that, if Paul were to visit some of our Western cities today, he would not think that the existence of differing, denominational congregations in the one street or vicinity was a denial of his doctrine that in one locality the Christians are one in the body of Christ; that is, they should in worship and witness, in fellowship and service, work together as the local manifestation of the universal body of Christ. It is perhaps true to say that his doctrine of the Church and churches cannot allow for competing (or even co-operative) congregations next door to each other or within a short distance of each other.

We can think of the Headship of Christ in two complementary ways. Firstly, Christ is the invisible Head of the Church, that is of all Christians and all Christian churches in the world. He is Head, as was noted above, because God appointed him as such (Eph. 1:22) and also because in his redeeming work he brought the Church into being. As the exalted Jesus, he sent out his disciples into the world, saying: 'Go, then, to all peoples everywhere and make them my disciples: baptize them in the name of the Father, the Son, and the Holy Spirit, and teach them to obey everything I have commanded you' (Matt. 28:19–20). We show our loyalty to our Head when we obey all that he has commanded us, especially the new commandment of his to love one another as he loved us (John 15:12,17). Secondly, Christ is the Head in that from him comes all the necessary power and means to make groups of people into true churches. In terms of the totality of churches in the world, and in terms of the one Church, Christ's body, his is the only spiritual reality which can make both a sinner into a saint and a collection of saints into a church. For by the Spirit he dwells in the Church and the churches. The Church and churches continue to grow in him until the purposes of God are fulfilled in and through them (Eph. 1:23).

To say all this is to say that the Lordship of Christ over his Church today challenges us to think seriously about how we understand and obey that Lordship in the local, national, and international situation in our complex Western society, taking into account, as we must, the denominational structures which we have inherited from the past (Rom. 14:7). How we should seek to draw churches together and what form the possible unions should take are difficult questions and, in the great freedom of action and thought which is so treasured by westerners, it is difficult to see any easy means of resolving the problems. Two things can perhaps be said. Let those who want to create new denominations or set up new local groups of Christians in contexts where already there is an abundance of congregations think most carefully about the Lordship of Christ over and in his Church and churches before they act. And let those who are members of existing local churches do all they can in prayer and gracious actions to help their congregation begin to function as a healthy body, so that it is in theory and reality a church of which Christ is Lord.

Jesus the Lord, as Prophet and Priest of his Church

Jesus was recognised as a prophet by his hearers (Mark 6:15; John 4:19, 6:14, 9:17). His words probed deep into the human condition and were authoritative in declaring the will of God. At times they related to the future, to the fall of Jerusalem, to the end of the age and the coming of the Son of Man (Mark 13; Matt. 25 etc.). He believed that after his exaltation the prophetic work which he had begun would be continued by the Holy Spirit. To the apostles he said, 'The Helper, the Holy Spirit, whom the Father will send in my name, will teach you everything and make you remember all that I have told you' and 'When ... the Spirit comes, who reveals the truth about God, he will lead you into all truth. He will not speak on his own authority, but ... will tell you of things to come' (John 14:26, 16:13).

But the Holy Spirit must speak through men even as he spoke through the prophets in the early Church (e.g. Agabus, Acts 11:28) and there was the gift of the Spirit known as the 'proclaiming of God's message' (1 Cor. 14:5). In (and through) all these gifts the exalted Jesus spoke prophetically to the young churches. Today the more usual method of his prophetic activity in terms of proclaiming the will of God is through settled church officers who are called in the New Testament 'bishops' or 'presbyters', 'pastors' and 'teachers'. In the faithful proclamation of the message of Scripture in terms which the congregations can understand and appropriate these servants of Christ and of the churches act as prophets of Christ, even as they are part of the gifts which Christ gives to his Church and churches.

There is also a sense in which each individual church, as a body, continues the prophetic work of Christ. This is suggested by Paul's statements in 1 Timothy 3:15 where he is explaining how Christians should conduct themselves in 'God's household', 'the pillar and support of the truth'. Here he is inviting Timothy to think of the churches throughout the world as being a series of pillars, all together holding up the truth of God so that all the world may see and hear it. Also he is asking him to think of the truth of God being defended in the world by a series of fortresses, all together preserving the truth from error and from heresy. It is a sobering thought that each Christian congregation or community is both a pillar holding up the truth in today's permissive society, and a bulwark defending it against those who would distort or change it.

For the teaching that the exalted Jesus is our heavenly Priest we turn especially to the Epistle to the Hebrews where he is portrayed (as we saw in chapter four) in terms of a priest of the order of Melchizedek. He offered his sacrifice for sins and then (using language based on the design of the Jerusalem Temple) passed through the heavenly courts until he reached the inmost sanctuary, the holy of holies, which is the presence of God. And there he permanently ministers as our Priest. The throne on which he sits as the Priest-King is a throne of grace and to that throne 'he opened for us a new way, a living way, through the curtain—that is, through his own body [offered in sacrifice]' (Heb. 10:19–20). As congregations and individuals we can approach that throne as those bearing prayers and sacrifices for we 'serve as holy priests to offer spiritual and acceptable sacrifices to God through Jesus Christ' (1 Pet. 2:5). Although he reigns as King, he receives our prayers and sacrifices as one who is aware of our human weaknesses (Heb. 4:14–16) and thus through his mediatorial power they become acceptable to God. Also as our Priest he represents our need and our cause to God, his Father (Heb. 7:25) who for love of his Son meets our every need.

In bringing the major part of this chapter to a close let us summarise the points we have made. The exalted Jesus is Head of the Church because the Father appointed him as such, but he is also the Head because the Church had its origin in his death and resurrection. As Lord he is the supreme and only ruler of the Church; his command and word are final. Also as Lord he alone supplies the spiritual life to his body. In his capacity as Prophet he speaks in the churches by the Spirit through those who preach, teach and rule. Finally as Priest he receives the prayers and service of his people and presents them purified to God the Father.

Lord of evangelism

Since Jesus is Lord over the nations and to him belongs all authority in the universe his command to his disciples remains: 'Go, then, to all peoples everywhere and make them my disciples: baptize them in the name of the Father, the Son, and the Holy Spirit, and teach them to obey everything I have commanded you' (Matt. 28:19–20). According to Luke's account the disciples are to be witnesses for Jesus Christ 'in Jerusalem, in all Judea and Samaria, and to the ends of the earth' (Acts 1:8). The Christian community, according to Peter, is 'chosen to proclaim the wonderful acts of God' who calls sinners out of darkness into his own marvellous light (1 Pet. 2:9).

From these passages and many others, it can be seen that the Church in the world has the joyous duty of proclaiming the gospel to all the nations. This means that in a given locality the major responsibility of evangelism belongs to the local body of Christ which worships there. With competing denominations in one area this may appear theoretical but the ideal must ever be before us, or else in the very making of disciples we shall perpetuate divisions and teach converts to accept these as inevitable and approved by God.

In terms of foreign missions the great aim must be to make disciples of Christ and to create local churches which are not dependent culturally, economically and theologically on a land far away, but which serve and glorify God in a way which is meaningful in terms of the local situation. Again the very existence of differing (and sometimes competitive) missionary societies can make this task appear impossible for it is easier to transplant our own external forms of the local fellowship of Christ than it is to create, under divine guidance, forms appropriate to a different context and culture.

The Lord who calls people, through the work of his Church, to be his disciples, also wants to bless them in terms of their human well-being. In his ministry in Galilee Jesus went about doing good in a variety of ways. And he told several parables which are a constant warning to us never to separate preaching from loving action towards people in need (see especially Matt. 25:31ff.). So the Lord of evangelism is also the Lord of love and the most lasting and effective Christian work is work in which the good news and the new life of the kingdom of God are inseparably joined.[3]

The Lordship of Christ over public worship

To conclude this chapter it will perhaps be useful to offer some thoughts on the way in which the Lordship of Christ makes demands upon the congregations who meet in his name. When Jesus was tempted by Satan in the wilderness one of the responses he made to Satan was in words taken from Deuteronomy chapter 6 verse 13, 'You shall worship the Lord your God and him only shall you serve' (Matt. 4:10 RSV). He told the woman with whom he talked in Samaria that the time was coming when 'by the power of God's Spirit people will worship the Father as he really is, offering him the true worship that he wants' (John 4:23). In order to achieve this spiritual worship which is pleasing to the Father the Lordship of Christ operates at two levels. It operates over the whole worshipping body setting for it standards for worship; and it operates over those who prepare and lead worship setting before them standards of spiritual excellency.

We consider first the Lordship of Christ over the whole congregation. Christians who meet together in worship meet primarily to worship God. In many old chapels the words, 'Give unto the Lord the glory due unto his name; worship the Lord in the beauty of holiness' (1 Chron. 16:29), are found written on the wall towards which all the seats face. We do not meet together to feel good (although this may happen); we do not come for a good sing (although we may have one). We come to render to God praise and thanksgiving for who he is and for what he has done and is doing.

We are required to worship with the Lord's people on the day of rest. Under the old covenant this was on Saturday, the Jewish Sabbath. Christians, celebrating the day of the resurrection of their Lord, take their day of rest on the Lord's Day when they meet around his table in order to be fed by him. They break bread to remember his broken body and they partake of the bread in order to symbolise that they live in the body of Christ, and are nourished by him.

Coming into the full experience of worship the Christian brings his total experience of life, all his hopes and fears, all his failures and successes, his concerns for others, his deepest longings and all these he offers with himself to God through Jesus Christ. This means he engages with others in confession of sin, in thanksgiving and in intercession for others. He, and those behind and in front of him, bring all because Christ is Lord of all and wishes to renew all. We come to give, to give everything to

God, and we do it with our sisters and brothers in Christ. As we give—and here is grace—God gives to us, through Christ our Lord, his grace and heavenly blessing. We thus go from the meeting with God and his people in the power of the Spirit to live for his glory in the world.

In order that our worship be of a true nature, the Lordship of Christ also operates over those who devise it, conduct it, and preach in it. This means that the minister or leaders must ensure that worship is addressed to God the Father through the Lord Jesus. This was the method of the apostles: 'Come to the Lord', wrote Peter (1 Pet. 2:4–5), 'come as living stones and let yourselves be used in building the spiritual temple, where you will serve as holy priests to offer spiritual and acceptable sacrifices to God through Jesus Christ.' The members of the church are a body of priests who together offer through Christ sacrifices of praise to the Father. The 'through Christ' is important. It is interesting to observe that in the Book of Common Prayer virtually every prayer ends with the words 'through Jesus Christ our Lord'. Though Jesus is near to us and loves us we still must treat him with reverence, for he is the Lord and the Messiah.

The leaders must also ensure that the contents of the liturgies or services which are used are based on the best understanding of the Scriptures which are available to them. This means in practice that they will be Trinitarian. The whole Scripture confesses to us that God is One, yet Three in One, and this divinely revealed Triunity of God is basic to the whole Christian understanding of worship and life. Thus the composition of services for public worship is not a task for amateurs or for people with little knowledge and experience. It is for those who have studied Scripture and have some knowledge of how Christians over the centuries have understood the demands of the Lord Christ in terms of worship. A time of worship is not an occasion for one person to force upon others his own pet aversions or idiosyncrasies. The ideal to which the composers of services and the preachers of sermons aim is that of excellence—sound theology, true spirituality and carefully chosen words and music. For the conveyance of the whole gospel we must use the best ideas, words and music available to us in our language and culture.

Another duty of our leaders is that they set forth Jesus Christ as both the Lord of all and the sole Mediator between God and mankind. He must not be belittled by our words concerning him or by our lack of reverence. So many popular choruses do not honour Christ for they cheapen him into someone who is on offer for any who want to take him. They portray him as it were as a chocolate in a box of chocolates which is on permanent offer. Just one example is, 'If you want joy, real joy, let Jesus come into your heart...' Jesus Christ is Lord and he certainly calls men and women to repent and believe in him, but he does not reduce himself to the level of being one among many possible solutions to the unhappiness of man. He is the supreme Lord of all; the only Mediator between God and men. It is a sad fact of life that many sincere, committed Christians who write choruses, while they have an abundance of enthusiasm, have little knowledge of the Scriptures or of Christian theology. In worship that is controlled by Christ the hymns and the choruses will reflect a full appreciation of him.

Finally, our leaders must ensure that public worship is edifying, that it builds up the body of Christ so that in and through the lives of this body God may be glorified.[4]

A PRAYER

O God, our Father, we worship you in the name of Jesus Christ. We praise you that he loved the Church and gave himself for her. We bless you that he is the Head of the Church and that from him comes the very life of the new humanity, his body. We thank you that he gives spiritual gifts to his people and that through human leaders he guides the churches. Help us, we pray, by your Spirit to offer to you such worship and service as is pleasing to you; direct us so to live and to work for you that the local church community will be seen by others to be the sphere in which your power and love dwells. Grant all this for the sake of our Lord Jesus Christ. Amen.

NOTES
[1] See R. Quebedeaux, *The New Charismatics* (1976).
[2] See further G. E. Ladd, *A Theology of the New Testament* (1974) and H. Ridderbos, *Paul, an Outline of his Theology* (1975).
[3] See further A. C. Kraus, *Go and Make Disciples* (1974) and *Let the Earth Hear his Voice*, ed. J. D. Douglas (1975).
[4] See further P. Toon, *Knowing God Through the Liturgy* (1974).

7 Jesus, Lord of the universe

WHEN A KING is crowned then he is said to rule over his subjects and over his territories. Thus the rule of the ascended and exalted Jesus over history and the Church follows from the idea of his heavenly coronation. In this chapter we are to look at teaching given by several writers in the New Testament which states not only that Christ, the Lord, rules the universe from the time of his coronation but that he was involved in its very creation. This latter assertion introduces us to what scholars call the doctrine of the pre-existence of Christ. There existed before the birth of Jesus of Nazareth a divine being who miraculously entered into a relationship with human nature through Mary. To this idea, and related ones, we shall turn in a later chapter. Here we must look at the teachings of Paul, John and the writer of the Epistle to the Hebrews concerning the relation of Christ to the universe.

Paul's teaching

On several occasions Paul expressed his commitment to the teaching of the Old Testament by insisting that 'it is God who brings everything into existence' (1 Cor. 11:12) and 'the earth and everything in it belong to the Lord' (1 Cor. 10:26, quoting Ps. 24:1). The same God who called the people of Israel into existence was the creator and preserver of the whole universe. This God had revealed 'both his eternal power and his divine nature' in creation and had thus given true knowledge of himself (Rom. 1:18ff.).

Under the guidance of the Holy Spirit and from various hints in the Old Testament (e.g. Prov. 8:22ff.) Paul came to see that God had created the world through Christ. An indication of the way Paul's thinking was developing is given in 1 Corinthians (written about AD 55) where he wrote: 'There is for us only one God, the Father, who is the Creator of all things and for whom we live; and there is only one Lord, Jesus Christ, through whom all things were created and through whom we live' (1 Cor 8:6). Here Paul, the former Jew, wholly committed to the famous *Shema* (Deut. 6:4: 'The Lord—and the Lord alone—is our God') is injecting into it his new understanding of the deity of Christ. The whole of the creation, animate and inanimate, is attributed both to the Father and to the *Kyrios*, the exalted Jesus, although the prepositions used—*ek* and *eis* in the case of the Father and *dia* of the Lord Jesus—suggest that the relation of each to the cosmos is not exactly the same. Nevertheless what we have here could be termed 'Binitarianism' (God is one but two in one) if we did not have other teaching to tell us that God is also Spirit, leading us to affirm that God is Trinitarian (three in one and one in three).

In the Epistles to the Ephesians and Colossians, written nearly a decade later, the cosmic role of Christ is closely associated with his redemptive role. The passage which is of primary importance and which therefore has been, and remains, the subject of much scholarly discussion, is Colossians chapter 1 verses 15–20. This passage was probably an early Christian hymn adapted by Paul in his effort to counteract the false teaching which had entered the church at Colossae.

What was the false teaching? It was the belief, common in the eastern half of the Roman Empire, that between God and man there was a great spatial gulf. In this was a series, in some order of hierarchy, of spiritual beings. These could be variously called 'aeons', 'elemental spirits', 'angels' or 'gods' (who inhabited the stars) and they were seen as affecting and even controlling the lives and destiny of mankind. The supreme God, who because of his very nature could not enter into space and time, acted in the world in and through these intermediary beings. Through them and their actions God was known on earth. In the Colossian heresy the Lord Jesus Christ was seen as one of these beings and so far from being unique he was regarded as one amongst several of the 'aeons' or 'angels'.

For Paul, ever since he had been grasped by Christ on the road to Damascus, there was only one Mediator 'who brings God and mankind together, the man Christ Jesus' (1 Tim. 2:5). No one, not even the archangels Gabriel or Michael, could take his place, for in him alone is salvation. 'The God who said, "Out of darkness the light shall shine!" is the same God who made his light shine in our hearts, to bring us the knowledge of God's glory shining in the face of Christ' (2 Cor. 4:6).

Following E. Schweizer and R. P. Martin[1] we can divide the hymn into three stanzas, which take up the themes of the creation, preservation and redemption of the universe.

The first of these is in Colossians chapter 1 verses 15–16: 'Christ is the visible likeness of the invisible God. He is the first-born Son, superior to all created things. For through him God created everything in heaven and on earth, the seen and the unseen things, including spiritual powers, lords, rulers, and authorities.' First of all we see that Christ is the 'image' of the invisible God, which the Good News Bible rightly here renders as 'visible likeness', for the Greek *eikōn* means 'the objectivisation of God in human life, a coming into visible expression of the invisible God' (cf. John 1:18, 14:9). Secondly, Christ is the 'first-born Son' and is superior to all created things. If the meaning here is decided on the basis of Proverbs chapter 8 verses 22 following, then Christ remains a creature (possibly an archangel), the one who was first made by God before he made the rest of the world. But if the whole context of Paul's thought is taken into account then Paul's meaning must be that Christ existed *before all creation*. To exist before all creation means that one has not been created. If all the creatures were created through this particular one then he cannot be a creature but must be a creator. So Paul's meaning appears to be that Christ was responsible with the Father for all that came into existence, all that we know now to be the massive cosmos in which we live.

We move on to verses 17–18a: 'Christ existed before all things, and in union with him all things have their proper place. He is the head of his body, the church; he is the source of the body's life.' Again we have a statement of the primacy of Christ over all things for he existed before all things. This leads on to an affirmation that Christ is also the One who sustains and who maintains the whole cosmos, keeping everything in its ordained place and function. Probably Paul's thinking (or that of the hymn he takes over) is informed here by Proverbs chapter 8 verse 30, 'I was beside him like an architect; I was his daily source of joy . . .' The Hebrew may also be translated 'I was at his side, a living link or vital bond, his daily source of joy'. Paul's doctrine that the power which causes the laws of nature to operate and guides the movement of the stars and planets in their courses is not, obviously, a scientific statement to be placed alongside Newton's theories or those of Einstein. Rather it is a profession of faith; but a profession based on a fact—provable only at the end of the age—that is, the Lordship of Christ. Paul is telling the Christians of Colossae that none of these intermediary beings has cosmic powers, only Christ possesses these. From the Christ who upholds the universe, his thought naturally flows to the same Christ as the supreme Governor of the Church, his body. The Christians of Colossae need to be told that no astral forces can control them, for their Lord is the one who not only created but also maintains the universe.

The third stanza is in verses 18b–20: 'He is the firstborn Son, who was raised from death, in order that he alone might have the first place in all things. For it was by God's own decision that the Son has in himself the full nature of God. Through the Son, then, God decided to bring the whole universe back to himself. God made peace through his Son's death on the cross and so brought back to himself all things, both on earth and in heaven.' Here the thought moves to Christ as the Second Adam who is the Head of a new humanity (cf. Rom. 5:12ff.) and thus the first-born among many brethren (cf. Rom. 8:2). The statement that in Christ is the full nature of God is to be read alongside the statement of Paul in Colossians 2:9 where he says that 'the full content of divine nature lives in Christ, in his humanity', which is a reference to the One who became Man and is now Jesus Christ, the Lord. The divine nature or essence which the false teachers claimed was mediated only through angels is, claims Paul, only mediated through Jesus Christ. He is the only one through whom the Father will reconcile the whole created order to himself, and the Father will do it on the basis of the redeeming work of Christ upon the cross.

So, in summarising the contents of this hymn adapted by Paul, we see that he believed in the pre-existence of Christ in whom dwells deity, that Christ (without his human nature) was the agent of creation, that Christ is the upholder of the cosmos, and that in Christ and his work there is a close link between creation, preservation and redemption.

There is another passage which we must examine, recognising as we do that it is a difficult passage and that scholars have not always agreed as to its meaning and interpretation. It is Ephesians chapter 1 verses 20–23:

> [God] raised Christ from death and seated him at his right side in the heavenly world. Christ rules there above all the heavenly rulers, authorities, powers, and lords; he has a title superior to all titles of authority in this world and in the next. God put all things under Christ's feet and gave him to the church as supreme Lord over all things. The church is Christ's body, the completion of him who completes all things everywhere.

The exaltation of Jesus Christ above the cosmic powers, his new name of Lord and his rule over the world are themes we have already studied. What is new here is in the last two sentences (verses 22b, 23) and concerns the relationship between Christ, the Church as his body and the cosmos. In Christ is the fullness of the divine nature

(Col. 2:9; Eph. 3:19). Christ is the Head of the Church constantly supplying it with the fullness of God's power and love. Christ is also Lord of the universe whose origin was caused by, and whose preservation is sustained by, the same power and love of God. Yet in the universe there is sin and there are demonic forces, resisting the Lordship of Christ, refusing to submit to the power and love of God. So it is in and through the Church that Christ is visibly setting up his kingdom and it is in and through the Church that his rule is visible and practically extending until at the end of the age that rule, by cataclysmic events, will become universal.

John's teaching

We are all familiar with the prologue of John's Gospel. Here the creation and redemption of the world are linked in the work of the *Logos* (Word):

> Before the world was created, the Word already existed; he was with God, and he was the same as God. From the very beginning the Word was with God. Through him God made all things; not one thing in all creation was made without him. The Word was the source of life, and this life brought life to mankind. The light shines in the darkness, and the darkness has never put it out. . . . The Word became a human being and, full of grace and truth, lived among us. We saw his glory, the glory which he received as the Father's only Son (John 1:1–5, 14).

Scholars have attempted over many years to ascertain the exact origin of John's use of this term *Logos*. Is it from

Greek, hellenistic sources or is it from Jewish sources (the Old Testament and Apocrypha) or from both? Without denying that the hellenistic usage was influential it is assumed here that the origins of the term are basically to be sought in the personification of the Word of God (Pss. 33:4ff., 107:20) and of the Wisdom of God (Prov. 8:22–31, and from the Apocrypha, Wisd. 7:22ff., 8:3, 9:ff.).

John teaches that the *Logos* is pre-existent, with God before the creation of the world; that the universe was created through the *Logos*; that the *Logos* is the light and life of men, preserving them and the world in which they live, and that the *Logos* took our humanity and became the Saviour of the world. In later chapters the *Logos* as Son is said to be one with the Father (John 14:8–11) and to share his glory (17:5). In other Johannine literature the same emphases are to be found. The *Logos*, the Son, is said to be the 'beginning and the end, the first and the last, the alpha and the omega' (Rev. 1:17, 22:13). He is not only the Creator but the One towards whom the creation is moving. Thus we see that the exalted Lord has a full cosmic role in Johannine theology, beginning with creation and moving through his role as the personal principle within creation (light and life) to his position as the person to whom all creation is moving (we may call this aspect teleological).

The teaching of the Epistle to the Hebrews

Here the important statements are in the first four verses:

In the past, God spoke to our ancestors many times and in many ways through the prophets, but in these last days he has spoke to us through his Son. He is the one through whom God created the universe, the one whom God has chosen to possess all things at the end. He reflects the brightness of God's glory and is the exact likeness of God's own being, sustaining the universe with his powerful word. After achieving forgiveness for the sins of mankind he sat down in heaven at the right-hand side of God, the Supreme Power (Heb. 1:1–4).

Seven facts about Christ are here affirmed. First, he is the agent of creation for through him God created the universe of space and time out of nothing. Secondly, he will possess all things in that as the Second Adam he is the Head of a new humanity and of a new creation; meanwhile he is ruling over a world which will pass away making room for the new heaven and earth for the new humanity. Thirdly, he is the effulgence, the brightness, of the glory of God. In and through Jesus of Nazareth the pure light of God shone into the hearts of men as well as revealing the character of God. In and through the exalted Jesus the light of God is now the light of men in that through Christ's body, the Church, it shines and is known. Fourthly, Christ is the 'image', the exact likeness of the invisible God (cf. Col. 1:15). Fifthly, Christ upholds, sustains and maintains the whole universe by his powerful commands (cf. Col. 1:17). Sixthly, Christ is the Saviour of men who in his historical death made purification for sins. Finally, Christ reigns as the exalted Lord.

Here, once more, we have a clear statement of the pre-existence of Christ; of his agency in the creation and preservation of the cosmos, of his sharing the deity of the

Father, and of the relation of his cosmic and redeeming work.

Creation and redemption in Christ

It is a basic belief of the writers of the New Testament that creation and redemption are one in Christ. This point is being made when what Christ achieved in his life, death, resurrection and ascension is called a new creation. This thought is the basis for the parallel between Adam and Christ, the Second Adam, (Rom. 5:12–21; 1 Cor. 15:45). Paul's expressions 'new creature' (Gal. 6:15; 2 Cor. 5:17; Rom. 6:4) and 'new self' (Eph. 2:15, 4:24; Col. 3:10) convey the same idea. Redemption fulfils the purpose of creation; redemption also brings into being the new creation and as such was in the mind of God from the beginning (Eph. 1:4, 9–10; Gal. 4:4; 1 Cor. 2:7). The content of this new creation is new life in Christ (John 5:26, 6:48, 14:6; 1 John 1:2, 5:11). The image of God planted in man at the first creation is being remade within the people of God (Col. 3:10). So the application of redemption to the individual sinner can be called a new birth, a being born into a new kingdom and a new creation (Rom. 8:14ff.; 1 Cor. 4:15; Gal. 3:26; Heb. 2:11; John 1:13, 3:6; 1 Pet. 1:3,23, 2:2; Jas. 1:18).

At the end of the age there will not only be a new people of whom Christ is Head, but God through Christ will make for them a new cosmos, and for this the whole creation is now waiting. 'All of creation', stated Paul, 'waits with eager longing for God to reveal his sons' (Rom. 8:19). The Christian community waits 'for what God has promised: new heavens and a new earth, where righteousness will be at home' (2 Pet. 3:13). This was what John saw in a vision as he was on Patmos; 'Then I saw a new heaven and a new earth. The first heaven and the first earth disappeared, and the sea vanished. And I saw the Holy City, the new Jerusalem, coming down out of heaven from God, prepared and ready, like a bride dressed to meet her husband' (Rev. 21:1–2). Yet before the new can replace the old God's purpose for the old must be accomplished. All things must be put visibly and demonstrably under the rule of Christ so that God can be all in all. This will mean confession by the whole of the old creation that Jesus Christ is Lord to the glory of the Father.

The cosmic Christ

The term 'the cosmic Christ' once found only in learned theological tomes, is now fairly generally known. The books, many of which have been in paperback, of Teilhard de Chardin, the Roman Catholic scientist and theologian, have helped to make the term more widely used. So also has the ecological crisis. Here is not the place to discuss Teilhard's view of the place of Christ in the cosmos. Yet it is perhaps the place to raise some of the questions which inevitably arise for Western educated Christians, especially those who know a little or a lot about physics and astronomy, when they seek to relate the biblical teaching about the exalted God-Man sustaining the small universe (as the ancients saw it) to the vast universe which we now know to exist. Before doing this it is worth saying that if we are to have any helpful development of doctrine in this aspect of the doctrine of Christ and his universe then the theologian will need to listen to and learn from the scientist concerning the nature of that universe to which he has to relate Jesus Christ.

To affirm that God, who is eternal and infinite Spirit, is the Creator and Sustainer of all that exists is a position which, taken the existence of God as proven, is a meaningful statement which most Christians (and indeed most Jews and Muslims) can understand. However, to affirm that Christ is the instrumental cause of creation, the goal of creation, and the immanent sustaining power of the created order is much more difficult to understand, even for Christians. And when we also affirm that the body of Christ, the Church, is at the centre or heart of the cosmos (Eph. 1:19–22) then we add a further dimension of difficulty!

When we speak of Christ in his cosmic relations are we thinking of him in his divine nature or in his human nature, or in both? Certainly in his role as the instrumental cause of creation we believe that only his divinity was involved. So are we to say the same of his work in preservation? But the teaching about Christ as the Head and Upholder of the universe is given, as we have seen, against the background of the exaltation of Jesus of Nazareth as Lord. How can humanity, even glorified humanity, be said to sustain the universe? If not humanity, then it appears that it must be divinity, but how can we separate the two in the one person of the exalted Christ? It is because of these problems, and others, that Teilhard speaks of a cosmic nature, which he sees as a third nature along with the humanity and divinity of Christ.

Can we any longer assume that ours is the only planet on which there is life? What would we say if in the next decade or so we found out that there was life on a planet of a galaxy of the Milky Way? What if we discovered an advanced civilisation millions of light years away? Would our understanding of Christ the Lord be sufficiently flexible to meet the demands of this new situation? Could we develop or expand our doctrine of the cosmic Christ to allow for an incarnation of the Son of God in that far away civilisation? Would it be the case that if we found life on another planet we would be able to see in the scriptural teaching of the cosmic Christ a greater depth of meaning and application than was possible in the days of Ptolemaic and Copernican science?

The thinker who would expound a theology of the cosmic role of Christ does not have carte blanche from which to start. He must start from a doctrine of *creatio ex nihilo* in order to be faithful to the biblical witness. God through Christ created the whole cosmos from, and out of, nothing. God is distinct from his world; he is transcendent. The world came into being through the utterance of his powerful Word and is sustained by the same powerful Word. In and of itself the cosmos has no meaning but it finds its meaning in its Creator and his purpose for it. For Christians the *Logos*, the Word incarnate, is the One from whom the cosmos derives its meaning. In their attitude towards the whole of creation they are to remember that Christ is the Lord and owner of it. And, as it belongs to him, it is to be treated in a way which is according to his will. To say this is of course to raise the whole question of ecology of which our generation is particularly conscious.[2]

But, returning to theology, the commitment to *creatio ex nihilo* means that those theologies which are based on what is known as process philosophy (usually associated with the name of Alfred N. Whitehead who died in 1947) must be rejected, despite their intellectual appeal.[3] To identify the *Logos* with the actual processes of the cosmos and of nature—the birth and death of stars, the development from simple to complex particles and biological evolution—is to reject the transcendence of God and to put God into the very cosmos which he is supposed to have made. This leads to bad science and bad theology. To divinise the cosmic process is to reject the God of the Bible. A better approach seems to be that of those who, in their concern to elucidate the true relation of science to theology, prefer to follow the insights of Albert Einstein and speak of the inherent rationality and comprehensibility of the created order.[4] This rationality which is a part of the nature of created things they then have to relate to the *Logos*, who for our sakes became man.

For most of us, these are lofty thoughts and all we are sure of is that we serve the Lord Jesus Christ whom we believe to have a cosmic role with cosmic functions. However, some of us may be the ones whom the Church of Christ needs in this generation to think through some of these difficult lines of theological enquiry in order that we can truly say that Christians do attempt to explain their faith in the contemporary world.

A PRAYER

This ancient 'Song of Creation' is taken from the Book of Common Prayer: though written from within 'a Ptolemaic universe' it is still useful.

O all ye works of the Lord, bless ye the Lord:
praise him and magnify him for ever.
O ye angels of the Lord, bless ye the Lord:
praise him and magnify him for ever.
O ye heavens, bless ye the Lord:

O ye waters that be above the firmament, bless ye the Lord;
O all ye powers of the Lord, bless ye the Lord:
praise him and magnify him for ever.
O ye sun and moon, bless ye the Lord;
O ye stars of heaven, bless ye the Lord;
O ye showers and dew, bless ye the Lord:
praise him and magnify him for ever.
O ye winds of God, bless ye the Lord;
O ye fire and heat, bless ye the Lord;
O ye winter and summer, bless ye the Lord:
praise him and magnify him for ever.
O ye dews and frosts, bless ye the Lord;
O ye frost and cold, bless ye the Lord;
O ye ice and snow, bless ye the Lord:
praise him and magnify him for ever.
O ye nights and days, bless ye the Lord;
O ye light and darkness, bless ye the Lord;
O ye lightnings and clouds, bless ye the Lord:
praise him and magnify him for ever.
O let the earth bless the Lord;
O ye mountains and hills, bless ye the Lord;
O all ye green things upon the earth, bless ye the Lord:
praise him and magnify him for ever.
O ye wells, bless ye the Lord;
O ye seas and floods, bless ye the Lord;
O ye whales and all that move in the waters, bless ye the Lord:
praise him and magnify him for ever.
O all ye fowls of the air, bless ye the Lord;
O all ye beasts and cattle, bless ye the Lord;
O ye children of men, bless ye the Lord:
praise him and magnify him for ever.

O ye people of God, bless ye the Lord;
O ye presbyters of the Lord, bless ye the Lord;
O ye servants of the Lord, bless ye the Lord:
praise him and magnify him for ever.
O ye spirits and souls of the righteous, bless ye
  the Lord;
O ye holy and humble men of heart, bless ye the
  Lord;

Let us bless the Father, the Son, and the Holy Spirit:
let us praise him and magnify him for ever.
Blessed art thou, O Lord, in the firmament of heaven:
to be praised and magnified above all for ever.

NOTES
[1] See E. Schweizer, *The Church as Body of Christ* (1964), pp. 64ff. and R. P. Martins, *Colossians* (1972), pp. 47ff.
[2] See further the Church of England Report *Man and Nature*, ed. H. Montefiore (1975) for a learned discussion.
[3] An example would be N. Pittenger, *God in Process* (1967).
[4] See for example, T. F. Torrance, *Space, Time and Incarnation* (1969) and W. Pannenberg, *Theology and the Philosophy of Science* (1976).

8 Jesus, Lord of all religions

IS JESUS CHRIST the only Lord? Can we, who live at the close of the twentieth century, claim that Jesus Christ is Lord of all religions? One is obliged to ask these questions because modern research and study in the field of world religions has immensely widened our knowledge and understanding of the major and minor religions of the world. The fact that there are many parallels between Christianity and other religions has been brought to light. No longer can one hold the view that Christianity is wholly true and all other religions are wholly false. Christians claim that Jesus is Lord; but, similar claims are made in other religions—for example, Krishna, Lord of the Hindus and Buddha, Lord of the Buddhists.

Krishna (the disguised avatar of God Vishnu) of Bhagavad Gita (the wellknown and much loved scripture of Hindus) is portrayed in Hindu art with a peacock feather in his hair (which is a symbol of his lordship) playing a flute to awake people from their sleep of 'maya' (illusion). Lord Sri. Krishna manifests himself as 'the Lord of all' in his avatar (an appearance of God into the world at a particular time, for a particular purpose, in a particular form). He reveals himself to Arjuna in these words of Bhagavad Gita: 'Although I am unborn, everlasting, and I am the Lord of all, I come to my realm of nature, and through my wondrous power I am born' (*Gita* 4: 6).

Hindus celebrate the birth of their Lord Krishna with pomp and gaiety. A Hindu devotee expresses his deep longing and wish to see Lord Krishna in these words of his prayer: 'Only one wish I have left in my life. I would like to see the Lord in the body ... When I was a boy, one day a holy man came into the house of my father. He told me much about the saints who had been honoured by seeing Lord Krishna ... He took my hand and prophesied that I, too, would see him.'

Buddhism is the predominant religion of the Far East. Siddhartha Gautama, the founder of Buddhism, was given the title Buddha which means 'the Enlightened One'. He is considered as 'the supreme Lord' by Buddhists. Many people look upon Gautama as a loving saviour. Modern educated Buddhists sing praises to Lord Buddha adapting Christian hymns, such as,

> *Glory, laud and honour*
> *To our Lord and King,*
> *This through countless ages,*
> *Men and Devas sing.*

and,

> *Buddha loves me, this I know*
> *For the Scriptures tell me so.*

Vivekananda (1863–1902), an eminent Hindu philosopher, considers Buddha as the greatest man the world has ever seen and, next to him, the Christ. M. K. Gandi, who is honoured as the 'father of India', once compared the teaching of Gautama Buddha with Jesus and remarked that the love for all creatures small and great, as found in Buddha's teaching, was lacking in that of Jesus.

Islam is the youngest of the world religions and post-Christian in time, being founded by Muhammad during the seventh century after Christ. Muslims look upon Muhammad as the last and greatest of the prophets with final authority while Jesus is viewed just as one of the great prophets.

The followers of these religions, besides making similar claims to those of Christians, frown at the intolerance and exclusiveness of Christianity. They will accept Jesus as 'a lord', one of the great teachers, but certainly not as the Lord of all religions. M. K. Gandhi expresses his view of Jesus saying,

> For many, many years I have regarded Jesus of Nazareth as one amongst the mighty teachers that the world has had . . . Of course, Christians claim a higher place for Jesus of Nazareth than as a non-Christian and as a Hindu I have been able to feel . . . Then, I can say that Jesus occupies in my heart the place of one of the great teachers who have made a considerable influence on my life.[1]

Vivekananda affirms his belief in the plurality of divine incarnation: 'The Word has two manifestations, the general one of Nature, and the special one of the great Incarnations of God—Krishna, Buddha, Jesus and Ramakrishna.'[2]

So, one begins to wonder whether the claim by Christians that Jesus is Lord above all religions can stand today. Furthermore, this claim is put to a more severe test than ever before as a result of some of the views being put forward from within the Christian tradition concerning the relationship of Christ and Christianity to other religions. Here we shall look briefly at four of these approaches.

Four approaches to other religions

In discussion among scholars and students there emerge several varieties of attitude to other religions which may be summarised as cultural relativism, epistemological relativism and teleological relativism, and all three may be classified under the heading 'relativity'. Cultural relativism generally presupposes that religions grow out of the culture. Thus Christianity is said to be the by-product of Western culture and Buddhism of South-East Asian culture. The claim involved in epistemological relativism is that it is impossible for us to know the absolute truth and so no one can claim that his religion is wholly true and other religions are wholly false. Thus Christianity is true only for Christians, and Islam for Muslims. Teleological relativism assumes that the end of all religions is one and the same though the ways to reach the end may differ. So, according to this view, the claim that Christ is the only way cannot be maintained.

SALVATION OF THE WHOLE HUMANITY

We can see that the three approaches mentioned above are represented in Professor John Hick's attitude to the other religions as provided in his book *God and The Universe of Faiths* (1973). His basic concern is 'salvation of the whole humanity'. If we say that Christ is the only way of life and salvation, what is the place of the millions of people who do not know Christ in God's plan of salvation? Do all non-Christians go to hell? Or are they all lost for ever? He believes that God whose nature is love cannot let man taste eternal death. He thinks that there is an inconsistency in the Christian understanding of God's love and his plan of salvation for all humanity. We

Christians say that God is a loving Father who desires the ultimate good and salvation of man. If this is so, he asks, how can God let man suffer eternal death? Thus making belief in Christ *the centre* of salvation of the human race presents a distorted picture of God's love for all humanity.

So, he tends to reject the view that salvation is *only* through Christ. He compares the Christ-centred salvation view with the old Ptolemaic system of the universe in which the earth was understood as the centre with other planets revolving around it. This false theory of the universe was changed by the Copernican system of the universe in which the sun was seen to be the centre with all the planets revolving around it, including the earth. In the same way that the erroneous Ptolemaic system of cosmology needed rejecting, so the doctrine that makes Christ the centre of salvation for humanity needs radically to be changed to a Copernican system of theology in which the divine reality, called by us 'God', becomes the centre. So, if God is the ultimate goal of all religions then non-Christians can reach this goal following their own ways. Further, along with this view he has a new understanding of Jesus Christ. He suggests that the doctrine that Christ is the *only way* of salvation for all mankind has been developed by the Church and it has insufficient historical foundation in the Gospels.

The following points can be made against the views of Hick.

1. His view has salvation for the whole of humanity at its centre; it is seen from the human point of view on what we may call the horizontal level. If God is truly the centre of the system of man's salvation, as he suggests, one has to view the whole system of man's salvation from *God's point*

of view. This means asking serious questions about how God has revealed himself.

2. He has failed to consider the day to day spiritual needs of man. Salvation of mankind is viewed only as an ultimate good, an eschatological ideal or event. Testimonies of converts from other religions to Christianity, in the past and at present, will establish the fact that Christ meets the deepest, contemporary, spiritual needs of man which other religions cannot satisfy.

3. His suggestion that the doctrine which states that Christ is the only way has no adequate historical foundation cannot be maintained because research and study in the field of biblical studies and archaeology continue to strengthen our belief in the authenticity of the New Testament accounts.

UNDER DIFFERENT NAMES

Professor Hick also holds the view that at the centre of all religions is the same essence. The divine reality is one but he is perceived as a personal God under different names. In other words, the divine reality is known by various names among various groups of people according to their cultural backgrounds. Essentially the religions of the world are not rivals: rather, they are different responses of man to the revelation of one divine reality. The differences in man's response are due to the variation of circumstances related to ethnic, geographical, climatic and historical factors.

Hick believes that God has been revealing himself through various men at various places at different times in the history of the world. Thus, he revealed himself through Isaiah and Amos to the Jews who lived in the eighth century before Christ. Yet Zoroaster revealed

God to the Persians, Confucius to the Chinese and so on. Behind all these revelations, the divine reality is the same. So, Jehovah, Allah, Krishna, Param Atman, Buddah and Jesus Christ are different names and personifications or concepts of the one ultimate reality. Hick accounts for the differences of truth in various religions by explaining that the full knowledge of the ultimate divine reality is beyond the reach of the human mind, and these differences are due to inadequate understanding on man's part.

We may raise three points against this position.

1. His view rests upon the mistaken belief that religion is a by-product of culture. According to this belief, one may consider the problem of the plurality of religions as not serious for, when the cultures of nations unite, the differences in religion will disappear.

2. According to Hick's view, God is basically seen as an abstract thing, rather than a living being; he changes with the change of culture of a particular community or nation. Man is therefore at liberty to form his own god according to his own cultural environment. In criticism it may be said that it is difficult to fit the concrete religions of the world into this scheme.

3. Hick's claim that Allah, Krishna and Jesus are partial images of the one 'unknown reality', with different names, cannot be maintained because Christianity alone is definite and specific in claiming that Jesus Christ is the full and true image of God. Muslims believe that Muhammad was only an apostle sent by God, 'the seal of the prophets' and not one in whom God is revealed to Muslims either partially or fully. Hindus believe that Krishna is one of the important avatars of Hinduism. Revelation of God, partial or full, is not at all found in the

purposes of any of her avatars. Christians alone claim that God is revealed to us in Jesus Christ. Further, there is a difference not merely cultural but qualitative between the life and teaching of Krishna and Jesus Christ, as well as in the demands they make on man.

This attitude to other religions represented by Hick is not new to us as this has been already expounded by Hindu Advaida philosophy (monism) by such teachers as Sri. Ramakrishna and Swami. Vivekananda during the later part of the nineteenth century. These philosophers created this theory and vehemently spread it to challenge the claim that Jesus Christ is unique. Nevertheless, some of them were impressed by the life of Jesus and admitted that there is something behind his life, something they want to imitate.

SALVATION HISTORY

The third Christian attitude to other religions which we examine is related to 'salvation history'. This view claims that God who is the Lord of history has a plan for the salvation of all mankind in human history. So, the other world religions constitute the way of salvation for their own adherents. Hans Küng, a leading Roman Catholic scholar, represents this approach clearly in his essay 'The World Religions in God's Plan of Salvation' in the book *Freedom Today* (1966).

In the first place Küng suggests that we can understand God's plan of salvation for other religions of the world only by looking from a 'theo-centric' (God-centred) point of view. At present we fail to do so, because we look from an 'ecclesio-centric' (church-centred) point of view which claims that there is no salvation outside the Church. Küng believes that the 'ecclesio-centric' view cannot be maintained because in God's plan of salvation there is no 'extra', only an 'intra'; no outside, only an inside; a centre, but no circumference.

Secondly, he views the 'salvation history' of the whole human race to be of two parts. These are the special salvation-history of the Church and the universal salvation-history of all mankind. Both of them find their origin, meaning and goal in the grace of God. An individual can find salvation within his own social environment and thus finally within his own religion which is socially imposed upon him. So, Küng suggests that we can speak of other religions as the 'ordinary' way of salvation and the adherents of those religions as Christians by 'designation'. In other words, the way of salvation for mankind outside the Church can be described as the 'ordinary' way and that within the Church as the 'extraordinary' way of salvation.

With regard to the teaching of other religions, Küng maintains the view that the religions of the world are in error; nevertheless in many ways they proclaim the truth of the true God. He says that this is evident from the way they recognise man's need of salvation and the need of God's grace. Though they proclaim the truth of Christ in a veiled way, there is much darkness in them because they fail now to recognise the living Christ who is *the* Truth. He goes on to explain that only Christ the living God who is *the* Light can eliminate the darkness in them.

Thirdly, he describes the relation between the Church and the other religions as follows: he claims, from a dogmatic standpoint, that the revelation made in Jesus Christ is absolute and that the gospel of Jesus Christ demands conversion to the true God through Jesus

Christ. However, the gospel does not demand renunciation of what is true and good in the other religions because the grace of God can transform the erroneous but sincere worship of a man into a true worship. The Church is an 'extraordinary' way of salvation. The Church is to serve the other religions and we can no longer consider her as the body of those privileged with salvation. But, the Church preaches the gospel so that men of other religions who are Christians by 'designation' may become Christians by 'profession'.

The following three points may be raised against the view of Küng.

1. Küng's view upholds 'universal salvation' at the expense of the uniqueness of Christianity. If other religions are 'ordinary' ways of salvation to their adherents why should there be an 'extraordinary' way of salvation which is through the Church? If adherents of other religions are Christians by 'designation', what need is there for them to become Christians by 'profession'?

2. Küng attempts to state the uniqueness of Christianity recognising the other religions as admissible ways of salvation. Unfortunately, this effort has the result of supporting indirectly the view of 'equality of all religions' which had been long proclaimed by Hindu philosophers.

3. This view limits the mission of the Church to the world to one of service. Evangelism which arguably is the primary mission of the Church is made optional and unnecessary.

REVELATION AND RELIGION

The fourth Christian approach to the other religions of the world, which we take up for discussion was set forth by Karl Barth in *Church Dogmatics* (vol. 2, 1938) and may be called 'exclusivism'.

Barth considers that religion is the one great concern of the godless man. He defines religion as 'unbelief' and thinks that it contradicts revelation which man has to apprehend by faith. He insists that revelation is the self-manifestation of God. It tells man the truth that God is God and that he is the Lord of man. Man cannot know and tell others of this truth apart from revelation. He has to abandon all his attempts to apprehend this truth by his own ingenuity because faith alone will enable him to apprehend it. He who understands this truth by faith is a genuine believer who comes to faith from unbelief.

In the first place religion contradicts revelation in that it is an activity in which man tries to know God by his own ways and methods. Religion is only an assumption because man has assumed the concept of God and created many different images of God according to his own imagination and means. Because man has rejected the knowledge of the true God in the revelation of himself in Jesus Christ in favour of his man-made religion, Barth says that 'religion is the concentrated expression of human unbelief'. He goes on to say, 'In religion man bolts and bars himself against revelation by providing a substitute, by taking away in advance the very thing which has to be given by God'.

Secondly, religion contradicts revelation in that man tries to justify and sanctify himself by his own means. Barth believes that revelation is *the act* in which God reconciles man to himself by grace. Man is helpless and unable to achieve this reconciliation because he is unrighteous and unholy and therefore condemned and lost. Man, who was created in the image of God became helpless because of his own deliberate disobedience of God. But, God in Jesus Christ reconciled man to himself and it was achieved once and for all. All the attempts of man to reach God have been replaced by Jesus Christ in whom we have our salvation and justification. A sinner becomes a justified sinner in Jesus Christ. But, in rejecting God's revelation man comes into direct opposition to him. Barth affirms 'God in his revelation will not allow man to try to come to terms with life, to justify and sanctify himself. God in his revelation, God in Jesus Christ, is the one who takes on himself the sin of the world.'

Barth thinks that it is 'heresy and unbelief' to understand revelation in the light of religion. So, he interprets religion in the light of the revelation of God in Christ Jesus, which is an historical event. Religion judged from the standpoint of revelation is man's anticipation of God's revelation which has taken place in Christ Jesus alone. When we view religion from this standpoint, we understand that no religion is true in itself, including Christianity. Revelation which is the self-manifestation of God is 'the truth beside which there is no other truth, over against which there is only lying and wrong'.

However, he says, a religion can become true not from within but from without, like a man who is justified not by his merits but from without by God's grace. In other words, only revelation can 'adopt and mark it off as true religion'. Christian religion is the true religion by virtue of this divine revelation. Thus Christian religion is true as against other religions because the righteousness and the judgment of God confront it in God's revelation in Jesus Christ. So, Barth views Christianity as a religion in which on the one hand there is nothing special, as a religion of unbelief; but on the other hand it is the true religion because in and through its proclamation of the one gospel the divine revelation of God in Jesus Christ is heard and received.

His view of the relation of Christianity with other religions is one of 'truth and falsehood'; that is, Christianity is true and other religions are false, for only in the proclamation of Christ is there truth from God.

We have no basic disagreement with the main thrust of Barth's argument and proclamation. As a true Christian, he honours and exalts Christ. Evangelical Protestants have tended to disagree with Barth primarily over his approach to Scripture.[3]

Jesus Christ remains Lord

Bearing in mind the situation concerning modern attitudes towards the other religions of the world, it is necessary to state the standpoint from which we shall consider the Lordship of Jesus over all religions. One possible way is to take one's stand outside the religions without being committed to one particular faith. Another way is to take a stand within one of the religions and begin with a clear, open acknowledgment of one's religious faith. We shall adopt the latter position because a Christian who is committed to the Christian faith cannot ignore his commitment and take his stand outside his faith. Some may object to this standpoint asking whether an unprejudiced treatment of the subject is possible especially when one is entering into the religious convictions of other faiths. However, a just treatment is possible because our stand is not within Christianity as a religion but within the revelation of God in Jesus Christ.

Let us, then, begin by making a humble but profound confession of our faith that Jesus Christ is the Lord. We claim that he is Lord of all religions for the following reasons.

GOD IS REVEALED IN THE PERSON OF CHRIST

Jesus Christ is Lord because the 'unknown reality' and 'ultimate mystery' whom we call 'God' revealed himself to the whole human race in the person of Jesus Christ. The Evangelist John writes, 'The Word became a human being and, full of grace and truth, lived among us. We saw his glory, the glory which he received as the Father's only Son' (John 1:14). God confronts us in and as a human personality—a Man who was born like us, lived, died and rose again, a Man who is living today for us. It was not the disciples who exalted Jesus as Lord, but they found God in Jesus and acknowledged him as their Lord. They could not possibly do any other than worship, as God, the exalted Jesus. His life, teaching, death and resurrection confirmed that God was in Jesus: he was the self-manifestation of God himself. He said, 'I am the way, the truth, and the life; no one goes to the Father except by me' (John 14:6) and, 'Whoever has seen me has seen the Father... I am in the Father and the Father is in me' (John 14:9, 10). No leader or founder of any other religion makes such a claim on human lives. Above all it was the resurrection of Jesus, an historical event, which confirmed more than anything else that Jesus was Lord to the disciples, who made a total surrender to his Lordship and willingly renounced everything in their lives to follow him. The same Jesus who is living today demands our total surrender to his Lordship.

The act of God coming into this world, which we know

as 'incarnation', is not a strange concept to other religions. Christians claim that Jesus Christ is God incarnate. Hindus believe in 'avatars' which convey a similar idea of God's appearances in this world. The most important avatars of Hinduism are Krishna (the avatar in the form of a charioteer) and Rama (the warrior king of Ramayana, an epic poem). Hindus accept Jesus and Buddha as avatars like any other avatars of Hinduism. However, the incarnation of God in Christ is unique in many respects. We list some points of difference below between the Christian understanding of incarnation and the Hindu idea of avatar.

The incarnation of God in Christ is historical whereas the historicity of Krishna and Rama are doubtful.

The incarnation of God in Christ is once and for all. As found in Bhagavad Gita, Krishna says that he manifests his being 'age after age', to protect the righteous and destroy the evil doers. 'For whenever there is a decay of righteousness, O Bharata, and a rising of unrighteousness, then I emit myself. In order to save the good, and to destroy evil doers, to establish righteousness I am born from age to age' (*Gita* 14:7,8).

The avatars of Hindu gods can be seen in various forms and figures, not restricted only to a human being. Christianity knows only one Incarnation which was in the person of Jesus of Nazareth.

The basic purpose of Christ's incarnation was to reveal God to man and to reconcile man and the world to God. No avatar of Hinduism or any other religion has a supreme purpose like that ascribed to Christ in Christianity.

Muslims find it rather difficult to accept the truth that God became man, identified himself with man and died for him. One of the major themes of the Qur'an, as scholars generally agree, is the righteousness of God. The idea of God as strict Judge includes the related truths, such as the punishment of the sinners, God's love for the penitent and guiltless and God's demand for an obedient response. The question that immediately comes to our mind is, how shall we know that God is righteous and compassionate? A young Muslim scholar says: 'There is only one way in which a fully personal and truly just God, such as Muhammad proclaimed, can realise his purpose in such a world as this. That is, by himself bearing the suffering of the world and the consequences of our transgressions. How can he be the just God of the Qur'an unless he suffers more than any man in total innocence?'[4]

This is exactly what God has done in Jesus Christ. Jesus Christ who was innocent and sinless was made sin for us. He suffered for the sin of the whole human race in his death on the cross. God's righteousness and compassion meet on the cross on which Jesus was crucified. St Paul says, 'God has shown us how much he loves us—it was while we were still sinners that Christ died for us! By his death we are now put right with God; ... we rejoice because of what God has done through our Lord Jesus Christ, who has now made us God's friends' (Rom. 5:8, 9, 11). Apart from the fact that God became man in Jesus Christ, we cannot understand God's righteousness and compassion. Jesus Christ is indeed Lord, having revealed this God of righteousness and compassion to us.

CHRIST FULFILS MAN'S SPIRITUAL NEEDS

Jesus Christ is Lord of all religions because, in revealing God to man, he fulfils and satisfies the spiritual needs of man which other religious ideas fail to do. In Jesus Christ we have a revelation which is absolute and final. Men all over the world have a deep innate longing to know God. Hinduism points out that man seeks 'the truth' (Hindus generally believe that God is Truth) because he wants to know 'the truth' and all his attempts to describe it result in 'neti, neti' ('no, no'). While other religions leave man helpless, Christ satisfies his longing to know God. Christ disclosed the truth of God so that we can comprehend and identify God's gracious activity throughout the universe. 'No one has ever seen God. The only Son, who is the same as God and is at the Father's side, he has made him known' (John 1:18).

The fundamental difference between Christianity and other religions is that in Christianity God seeks man to satisfy his longings whereas in other religions man seeks God in vain. God's revelation in Christ is complete because Christ completes the incomplete knowledge of God in other religions. No other source of revelation is necessary or possible if one has Christ. Partial revelation of God found in other religions, given to them by God's grace through his creation, was completed by the incarnate Christ. So full knowledge of God is only found in Christ. Adherents of other religions come to the full knowledge of God when they submit themselves to the Lordship of Jesus Christ. A Japanese monk who became a Protestant Christian says, 'Nothing of the best in Buddhism is lost in Christianity, although there is a radical breach between Christianity as a revealed religion and Buddhism as a mere product of human reflection.'

Jesus Christ fulfils man's longing to have fellowship with a personal loving God. As Lord he came into this world to restore the broken relationship between God and man. Man found it impossible to reach God. He was totally helpless until Jesus Christ came into the world to make it possible for man to have personal fellowship with God. Jesus Christ demonstrated God's great love for the whole human race in the sacrifice of his life in giving himself to be crucified on behalf of man. This voluntary act of giving his life for man, challenges people everywhere to submit to his Lordship. No other religion demonstrates God's love in such a recognisable way. In Hinduism, for example, the concept of the love of God for men emerged late against her traditional teaching. Professor S. C. Sengupta[5] recognises this difference in these words: 'One important point of difference between the two, however, is that the latter [Christian theism], unlike the former [Hindu theism] focuses on the forgiving and redeeming character of the divine love.' The forgiving and redeeming love of God is freely available to man by God's grace through Jesus Christ. Bhagavad Gita describes how man begs for God's grace and love. The gospel proclaims that it is in Jesus that he can find grace and love.

Buddha taught people to love all creatures of the world and the theme of many great men's teaching has been love. But, it was only Jesus who both taught and exhibited God's love in his life. Accepting God's love through Jesus Christ brings joy and peace in one's life here and now. This is not to say that one who accepts Jesus as his Lord is free from sickness, sorrow and other calamities of life. But, it is true that joy and peace, in times of sickness, sorrow and trouble will abide in his life. Further, it gives the real meaning and purpose for one's life, here and now, as well as hope for the future.

There are four qualifying remarks which need to be

made in claiming Lordship for Jesus Christ over other religions of the world.

We do not deny the partial knowledge of God found in other religions. But we do state that this partial knowledge of God is insufficient in itself to give man a satisfying relationship with God.

We avoid any suggestion that he who does not know of, or does not submit to, the Lordship of Jesus will be eternally punished. But we do say that such people do not know the real meaning of life and probably miss the privilege of having eternal fellowship with God.

We affirm that, out of love and concern for others who do not accept the Lordship of Jesus, the message that Jesus is Lord of all religions should be made known through the life and preaching of every Christian.

We urge that all people everywhere need to submit themselves to the Lordship of Jesus Christ, by believing that he is God incarnate.

A PRAYER

O God our Father, who on the day of Pentecost and afterwards enabled your Spirit-filled people so to bear witness to their exalted Lord that men of different races heard the good news in their mother tongue; baptise your Church today with the same Spirit of power that she may fulfil her mission to preach the gospel to the whole creation and all the peoples of the world may learn of Christ in their own language and thus become the subjects of his kingdom, for in his name we pray. Amen.

NOTES

[1] *The Message of Jesus Christ*, ed. A. T. Hingorani (1963), pp. 41–2.
[2] Quoted in M. M. Thomas, *The Acknowledged Christ of the Indian Renaissance* (1969), p. 122.

[3] See further C. Brown, *Karl Barth and the Christian Message* (1967).
[4] Quoted by S. Barrington-Ward, 'The Personal Centre', *Theological Renewal*, No. 5 (1977), p. 9.
[5] S. G. Sengupta, 'The misunderstanding of Hinduism', *Truth and Dialogue*, ed. J. Hick (1974), p. 102.

9 The exalted Jesus and the Creeds

THE PREVIOUS CHAPTERS have been written from within the belief that God is one, yet three in one, and that the exalted Jesus is God and Man in one Person. This way of speaking about God and Christ did not occur in the Church either easily or quickly, even though it is presupposed today in our services of worship and in our theology. Between the writing of the New Testament in the first century and the expression by the Christian leaders in the fourth and fifth centuries (which was repeated by the Protestant Reformers of the sixteenth century) of what is usually called the Catholic Faith (One God in Trinity) there was a complex process of development or explication of doctrine. It is our task in this chapter to notice how the biblical doctrine of the exalted Lord was expressed in terms drawn from non-biblical sources. For, as the famous German historian, Adolf von Harnack, has written, 'Confession of the Father, the Son and the Spirit... is a development of the belief that Jesus is the Christ and Lord'. He is, of course, thinking of the development of dogma within the Church in the period following the work of the apostles.

Nicea and Chalcedon

The relationship of Jesus Christ to God the Father is the theological theme which lies at the heart of the Nicene Creed, a confession of faith used by many churches in Sunday worship.

> I believe... in one Lord Jesus Christ, the only-begotten Son of God,
> Begotten of his Father before all worlds,
> God of God, Light of Light, very God of very God,
> Begotten, not made,
> Being of one substance with the Father,
> By whom all things were made:
> Who for us men, and for our salvation came down from heaven,
> And was incarnate by the Holy Spirit of the Virgin Mary,
> And was made man,
> And was crucified also for us under Pontius Pilate.

Framed originally by the Council of Nicea (325) and finalised by the Council of Constantinople (381) the Creed was composed primarily to answer the challenge of Arianism. This heresy, like that of the modern Jehovah's Witnesses, claimed that Jesus of Nazareth was the incarnation, not of God himself, but of a superior angel or spiritual being.

In the churches of the fourth century there was no doubt that the One called Father is God. He is 'I am who I am' (Exod. 3:14), the Creator of the universe. However, the sense in which Jesus Christ is God or related to God was less easy to determine. All admitted that he was the unique Servant of God; all were happy to call him the Son of God, and all were content to praise him in the liturgy on Sundays. But was the title 'Son of God' merely a courtesy title or was it a statement that the same divine reality or being that is God is to be found in Christ, the Lord?

Arius (c. 250–336), a presbyter of Alexandria, maintained that Son of God was definitely a courtesy title and that Jesus Christ was the incarnation of the highest of all the angels, whom God the Father sent as his servant to be the saviour of the world. When Jesus had finished the work given to him then God rewarded him by raising him from death and exalting him into heaven. Arius was a good teacher and very influential. He put his doctrine that Jesus is the incarnation of a created being into popular form for the less educated in what we today would call choruses. One of them went 'There was a time when Christ was not'. Here he declared that God created the angels and then created the world. Christ was the incarnation of the first angel and so he did not exist eternally with God.

Arius believed, as thousands still do today, that the most important thing to make clear was the truth that God is one and only one who cannot be more than one. Therefore Jesus Christ cannot be God even though he is the highest possible creature under God. Arianism challenged, not the functions of Jesus Christ, but the traditional understanding within the Church that Jesus Christ was the unique God-Man, worthy of the worship which alone belongs to God.

The question which Arius forced upon the thinking of the leaders of the Church was, 'Is Christ the Son of God in the full sense, sharing the same divine nature as God the Father?' The answer that came from the Church was in the words quoted above. The statements which explain the relation of Jesus Christ to the Father do not contain any biblical verses for the simple reason that Arius and his friends were always ready to quote the Bible. The bishops who framed the Creed had to go to the world of

Greek philosophy to find a word which summarised what they believed to be the total meaning of the whole biblical teaching. The term they used was *ousia* which means 'essence' or 'being' or 'substance': Jesus Christ is 'of one substance with the Father'. To say that three pieces of wood share the same *ousia* is to say that the wood which constitutes all three pieces is exactly the same, be it oak or elm or any other type. Jesus Christ possesses the same eternal being as the Father. He is *homoousios* (of the same essence) with the Father.

Arius saw the problem as an 'either or'. Either Jesus Christ is God or he is not God and since God is one he cannot be God. The Church answered, 'God is one and Christ is God'. The unity of God had to be considered in a new way. The Christians knew God both through revelation of Scripture and in experience as Father, Son and Holy Spirit. The God whom they served had three different ways of being God and so they confessed God as three in one and one in three. In the Nicene Creed the deity of the Spirit is thus confessed:

> I believe in the Holy Ghost,
> The Lord and giver of life,
> Who proceedeth from the Father and the Son,
> Who with the Father and the Son together is worshipped and glorified,
> Who spake by the Prophets.

And in Christian worship the basic theme is always, 'Glory be to the Father and to the Son and to the Holy Spirit'.

The relation of the exalted Lord Jesus to God the Father and to the Holy Spirit is that he shares with them the divine *ousia*. Unlike the Father and the Spirit the exalted Lord has also a glorified humanity joined to his eternal deity.

The Council of Nicea faced the question, 'If the Father and the Son are both God how can God be one?' The answer was the exposition of the doctrine of the Trinity of God. The next set of probing questions which the Church faced surrounded the general question, 'If Jesus Christ is both God and man, how can *he* be one?' The relationship of the two internal aspects of Jesus Christ, his humanity and his deity, is the problem to which the Council of Chalcedon addressed itself in 451. Its solution was incorporated into the Quicunque Vult (the Athanasian Creed), which has been recited for centuries in the Church of England and was also used as the framework of doctrine for the confessions of faith produced by the Reformers and their successors.

The kernel of the document produced by the bishops at Chalcedon is found in two paragraphs. The first insists that Jesus of Nazareth, the Son of God and Lord of men, is a unity. It reads:

> We all with one voice teach that it should be confessed that our Lord Jesus Christ is one and the same Son, the same perfect in Godhead, the same perfect in manhood, truly God and truly man, the same consisting of a rational soul and a body: of the same substance [*homoousios*] with the Father as to his Godhead, and the same substance [*homoousios*] with us as to his manhood: in all things like unto us, sin only excepted: begotten of the Father before the ages as to his Godhead, and in the last days, the same, for us and for our salvation, of Mary, the Virgin, who is the God-bearer as to his manhood.

While he is one, Jesus Christ, both on earth and now in heaven, has a double solidarity, with God and with humanity.

The second paragraph is of greater importance:

> One and the same Christ, Son, Lord, Only-begotten, made known in two natures without confusion, without change, without division, without separation: the difference of the natures having been in no wise taken away by reason of the union, but rather the properties of each being preserved, and both concurring into one Person, not parted or divided into two persons but one and the same Son and Only-begotten, the divine Logos, the Lord Jesus Christ.

This may appear complicated but the bishops desired to preserve the true faith of Christ and thus refused to make things out to be simpler than they really were. The four phrases beginning 'without' need comment. First, in Jesus Christ there was and is both deity and humanity, a divine and a human nature, but they are not so joined as to be confused together. Jesus was not a kind of half-way being between God and man; he was both God and man. Secondly, the two natures were not changed by their union. We are not to say that when Jesus was born God was changed into a man and we are not to say that when Jesus ascended into heaven a man was changed into God. Thirdly, though he has two natures he is not two individuals functioning inside one casing of flesh for the two natures work together in perfect harmony. Finally, in Jesus there is a permanent union of the two natures: there is no separation. This statement from the Council of Chalcedon does not solve the mystery of the Person of

Jesus Christ, the Son of God. Rather it builds walls in which further reflection can continue around the truth that Jesus is both God and Man. Jesus Christ possesses full and perfect divinity; he also possesses full and perfect humanity; in him there is a perfect union of God and man, and with two natures he is one Person, one Christ.[1]

One difference which immediately strikes us as we compare the biblical teaching with these statements from the Councils of Nicea and Chalcedon is that while the biblical material describes primarily the functions of Christ the Lord and his loving relationship with the Father, the ecclesiastical teaching draws out the implications of this in terms of the true being or essence of Christ. In the New Testament Jesus is portrayed as the Saviour of his people, the Mediator of a new covenant, the Reconciler of God and man, the Intercessor who prays for the Church, the Lord who governs and upholds the universe, the King who rules the nations, and the Judge who examines all men. At the same time it is assumed that he comes from God, that God works in him and that he and God are one in purpose and nature. The ontological status of Christ, that is his nature and essence, only emerges through the explication and declaration of his functions as Messiah and Lord. There is, however, no sustained ontological enquiry into the exact nature of the relationship of the Father and the Lord Jesus, or between the Father, the Son and the Holy Spirit. Neither is there an enquiry into the way in which Jesus was both God and Man. Yet, since the Bible is the book which describes God's activity in saving mankind, it is not surprising that the Christ of the Bible is portrayed primarily in functional terms. It is also not surprising that once the Christian faith became a force within Greek and Roman culture questions should arise concerning the ontological status of Jesus the Lord.

Scripture and creeds

Many Christians are confused not only concerning what value to put on the ancient creeds (and also later confessions of faith) but also concerning what relation they bear to Scripture. This being so, it will perhaps be helpful, making use of a few analogies or analogical models, to suggest ways in which we can think of the relation of creeds to Scripture and Scripture to creeds.

Consider first of all the growth of a seed into a plant or of an acorn into an oak tree. It has been suggested that the growth of biblical teaching into creedal teaching is of this type. The contents of the creeds are the culmination of the growth of theology, the first principles of which are written in Scripture. This model has both strengths and weaknesses. It emphasises the close connection between biblical and creedal teaching thus correctly representing the intention of the makers of the creeds to represent the principles of Scripture correctly. On the negative side it gives the impression of unified and harmonious growth and does not do justice to the fact that new ideas and terminology were imported by the bishops into the creeds.

Consider, secondly, the mental activity of 'calling to remembrance'. In Hebrews 10:3 we read that by making the annual sin offerings in the Temple the Jews called to remembrance their sins. In the Christian Eucharist, the Lord's Supper, Christians re-enact the whole action of the Last Supper in the upper room—they break bread and pour wine in recollection of Jesus and of what he did in his sacrificial death. There is a kind of making present, in the liturgical act, of the effectiveness of what was done once for all upon the Cross. So it can be said that the bishops who met at Nicea and Chalcedon were calling to remembrance, in order for it to have relevance in their situation, the whole teaching of the Scriptures concerning the Lord Jesus Christ. They called into their thinking and theological reflection the events and teaching given centuries earlier and recorded in the Bible in order to be able to confess and proclaim that same teaching in a new context and in a new framework of thought.

Consider, thirdly, the development of a site by a land developer. He buys a piece of land, clears it and using various skills and machinery he develops it so that where there was only once a field or dilapidated property, there arises a new block of offices. So the development might include demolition, excavation, building and, within all this, the personal activity of the men employed by the developer. When theologians produce a statement of doctrine they are doing something like this. They begin with certain teaching (for instance Arianism) and they demolish it but use that upon which it is based, the contents of Scripture, in order to build a new building which is more securely attached to its foundations. Another way of using this model is to see the theologians as developing the contents of Scripture in that on the principles of Scripture they build an edifice which rises out of, and from, the Bible although it is not part of it. It rises up from the Bible into a different thought-world which, in the case of the Nicene bishops, was a Greek culture.

Consider, finally, the work of Michelangelo in the creation of his great piece of sculpture which we know as

'David'. We are told that the sculptor went out of the city to a quarry where he personally chose a large piece of rock in which he could visualise what he wanted to create. This rock was then brought by men and mules to his workshop. Then with ideas in his mind and chisel in his hand he produced his masterpiece. Here we have what we may term the interaction and fusion of the constituent elements with the structured element. The structured element is the piece of rock, whose shape has been determined by various forces within nature. The constituent elements include the men and mules who brought it to the workshop but they are primarily the ideas and energy and tools of the master sculptor himself. This model helps us to see how one theologian in a council (as Athanasius of Alexandria) creates doctrine. The structured element from which he works is the teaching of Scripture, fashioned as it is in the minds of Matthew, Mark, Luke, John and Paul. To a lesser extent it is also the writings and confessions of faith of bishops and theologians who have already written about Christianity. The constituent elements are the realities in the situation by which he is conditioned or to which he has to relate. These include the problems raised by the heretic, the philosophical concepts available in the language of the theologian and a variety of other factors.

A further illustration of this model which brings out the corporate activity of a team of theologians is that of the production line in a factory. Various materials, usually semi-processed, enter the production line at one end. As they move along the line they are fashioned, moulded or pressed by men and machines until the final product—a car or refrigerator perhaps—emerges at the end of the line. The structured elements—metal, glass, plastics—interact with and fuse with the constituent or structuring elements—men and machines—in order to produce something. So theologians in a council take structured materials from the Bible and from the traditional teaching of the Church and this they mould in order to make it meet the emergency or the problem to which they are addressing themselves.

Perhaps if we take three models together, those of calling to remembrance, developing a site and the interaction and fusion of the constituent and structured elements, we shall gain some understanding of the historical processes which help to bring Church dogma into being.[2]

These models also help us to understand the task of the theologians of the Church today as they are called to create for us new doctrine which, while being faithful to Scripture and to the best insights of the Church in the past centuries, is nevertheless addressed to contemporary theological problems and makes use of modern ideas which are 'baptised into Christ'. An example of a contemporary need, which was mentioned in chapter seven, is for a doctrine of the cosmic Christ.

As the writer is well aware, the discussion in this chapter raises such questions as: What is the relation of creed to Scripture in terms of authority within the Church? What relevance has a fourth or fifth century creed to the twentieth century? While an ontological approach to creedal affirmation was necessary to the bishops at the Councils of Nicea and Chalcedon, is it essential today in Europe or in Asia? These need to be faced and freely discussed by educated Christians; but unfortunately to discuss them here would be to move out of the limited aim of this short book.

A PRAYER

From the Book of Common Prayer

Almighty and everlasting God, who has given unto us thy servants grace by the confession of a true faith to acknowledge the glory of the eternal Trinity, and in the power of the Divine Majesty to worship the Unity; we beseech thee, that thou wouldest keep us steadfast in this faith, and evermore defend us from all adversities, who livest and reignest, one God, world without end. Amen.

NOTES

[1] See further J. N. D. Kelly, *Early Christian Doctrines* (1976) and H. E. W. Turner, *Jesus the Christ* (1976).

[2] For a study of the factors behind the Nicene theology see M. F. Wiles, *The Making of Christian Doctrine* (1967).

10 Jesus, my Lord

WE RETURN NOW to the point which was made in the first chapter. It is in response to the gracious call of God made in the proclamation of the gospel that the repenting sinner confesses that 'Jesus Christ is Lord'. Though perhaps not conscious of divine help, he makes this confession assisted by the Holy Spirit who now comes to dwell in his heart, for as Paul teaches, no person can say that Jesus is Lord but by the Holy Spirit. The believer now looks to Christ as the Way, the Truth and the Life, finding in him alone, either immediately or over a period of time, the key to the full meaning of life here on earth. The relationship between the believer and his Lord is personal. Certainly all kinds of words, images and sentences are used to describe and explain this relationship, but, at its heart, it is the communion of a finite being with an infinite being. Though what the Christian believes about Christ and about his duties as a Christian are important, the heart of the Christian faith is this relationship, a personal relationship of a Master and his slave, of a Teacher and his disciple, or a heavenly Friend with his earthly friend. This is why prayer is so important, for in prayer there is communion between Christ and the one who prays.

The Lord of the cosmos, human history and the Church is my Lord because by faith I am united to him. This Lordship of Christ sometimes operates directly at the personal level as Christ and his disciple commune with each other and relate to each other in life. At other times the Lordship operates through the body of Christ. What is implied by this latter assertion will become clearer if we recall what happens when a person becomes a Christian and is baptised into Christ. Through union with Christ he enters into a relationship with God, the Father, whom he may now call 'Father'. The Spirit of the Father and the Son witnesses with his spirit that by grace he is a child of God. Yet the relationship vertically with God also causes to come into being a horizontal relationship with other Christians. He becomes a subject of a kingdom, the kingdom of Christ; he is made a citizen of a new city, the New Jerusalem; he is born into a family, the family of God; he is given membership of a new race of people, the new humanity under the Second Adam; he is made a membrane in a body, the body of Christ; he becomes a priest in a royal priesthood; he is built as a stone in a temple, the temple of the Holy Spirit; and he, with others, is a bride, the bride of Christ. So the Christian knows God directly at a personal level and also in a corporate sense, through his brothers and sisters.

It is probably true to say that for most western Christians (and this includes Roman Catholics) the conscience is the final court of appeal. Other people may advise me but in the end I must decide whether to take or not to take a specific action, to do or not to do a specific thing, to say or not to say a specific sentence. Yet, since the Christian is bound both directly to God in Christ and also the Church of Christ his conscience must be tutored by both these personal bonds in order that he can make a decision which is truly according to the Lordship of Christ.

Obviously the contents of Holy Scripture will be the chief means, if not the only primary means, by which both the whole Church and the individual Christian will be made aware of the nature and demands of Christ's rule. So the question arises for the individual Christian, as he lives in a society where the rights of the individual are much emphasised, how do I approach Scripture and how do I interpret it so that I may know the mind of Christ my Lord? From this basic question related ones spring up. Do I read Scripture in isolation and decide for myself what it means? Or does my God-given relationship with the household of faith place certain obligations upon me? Surely my relation to Christ and his people means that my approach to the source of the knowledge of Christ's commands is guided by, enriched by and checked by the help I get from the local church and the Church in general.

This help will come through the spoken word in sermons, study groups and counselling and through such written sources as commentaries on the Bible, theology books, books of prayers and Bible reading notes. From these sources, over a period rather of years than of days, my conscience is informed through my mind both what the original language of Scripture means and how learned and godly Christians have understood it over the years of the existence of the Church. Therefore I can read Scripture with more understanding and thus know more clearly what are the demands of Christ upon me and upon my family in today's scene.

The danger is that unless I relate to my brothers and sisters in Christ I may well read *into* the text of Scripture what my imagination and feelings want to find there, rather than reading *out* of Scripture what God wants me to know and to do. Certainly what concerns me, if I am of age, I must finally decide, but my decision is to be made as a member of the body of Christ, which has historical as well as existential roots and connections.

The radical ethic

We hear and read of radicals, usually 'leftists' of one kind or another, who challenge the status quo of our society by their life-style and their propaganda. It is generally recognised that the implementation of their proposed radical systems of government and structures for society would dramatically change the nature of society as we now know it. What is less recognised, even within the churches, is that the morality, private and social, demanded by the Lord Christ is radical both in its nature and contents. It probes to the very centre of our beings and makes all-embracing demands upon us.

Normally when we think of moral standards we think of that which we do and say. To steal, to tell a lie, to inflict injury and to be unfaithful to a partner we know to be wrong. We know it to be wrong despite much modern literature, many modern films and plays which tell us a different story. But what goes on in our thinking as we sit in a chair or travel on a city train, or how we feel and what we desire and imagine as we lie awake in bed, these thoughts, feelings and imaginations we commonly regard as private, having little to do with others or with morality. We think of a person as good if he is kind, considerate, faithful, honest and patient. And it comes as a bit of a shock to us when we visit an elderly person who has been known as a good person and from whose mouth there now flows from time to time a filthy stream of language. Psychiatrists can easily explain this but the Christian suspects that here, over the years, there has been an area of life suppressed rather than renewed and over it Christ has not been allowed to rule as Lord and to cleanse as Saviour. Christ the Lord demands to be Lord of thoughts and emotions as well as Lord of words and actions.

In the Sermon on the Mount Jesus clearly taught that purity of heart and mind is both an obligation and the source of true joy. 'Happy are those who are humble; they will receive what God has promised ... Happy are the pure in heart; they will see God' (Matt. 5:5, 8). Later, in 'filling up' the meaning of the Old Testament Law he emphasised the important point that the thoughts behind our words and actions, being observed and known by God should be as much under his rule as the externalisation of them. To harbour anger against another human being, to attend worship hating a brother, to desire to have sexual relations with a person who belongs to another, and to want revenge for injuries received are all internal attitudes which stand under the condemnation of Christ the Lord. The call is not to 'love your friends, hate your enemies', but, rather, to 'love your enemies and pray for those who persecute you' (Matt. 5:43–4). The Christian ideal, to which all are called to strive, is the perfect life of love, and love is attitude and action and word. Love to God and love to human beings is the Christian life-style. To judge and condemn others, loving only those who are near or dear, is the way of the world. To love and care for others, both strangers and enemies and those we encounter daily, is the way of Christ, and it is only possible when people build their lives on a sure gospel foundation. This is the force of the parable told by Jesus about building the house on the rock (Matt. 7).

Often it has been remarked that the standards of the Sermon on the Mount are too high for the most committed Christian to attain, even when encouraged by his brothers and sisters in Christ. This is true. They always stand before the Christian and before the Church as the goal towards which, out of love for Christ, we are to move. By the power of the Spirit we are enabled gradually to conform towards the purity of heart and integrity of word and action required of disciples of the kingdom of God. Even the mature Christian has to press on towards the perfection to which he is called as he grows daily in the grace and knowledge of God.

The centrality of love, that pure emotion and attitude which is the gift of God to the Christian believer, is described by Paul in 1 Corinthians chapter 13. 'Love is patient and kind; it is not jealous or conceited or proud; love is not ill-mannered or selfish or irritable; love does not keep a record of wrongs; love is not happy with evil, but is happy with the truth. Love never gives up; and its faith, hope and patience never fail.' John wrote to the churches telling them that 'whoever loves his brother lives in the light' (1 John 2:10). Paul told the Philippian Christians to fill their minds 'with those things that are good and that deserve praise; things that are true, noble, right, pure, lovely, and honourable' (Phil. 4:8) which is another way of talking about purity of heart. This reminds us of the dramatic illustration provided by Jesus of plucking or cutting out one's eye in order to prevent that eye being the occasion of allowing into the mind sensations which lead to impure thoughts and desires (Matt. 5:29). We all know from experience that certain activities, ranging from reading certain glossy magazines to playing golf at the weekend, are the means whereby the wrong ideals become the focus of our thinking and feeling. These, said Jesus, are to be avoided; they may be lawful but they are not expedient if our aim is to live by Christ's standards.

Christ is the Lord of every department of the Christian life. One cannot serve two masters; the allegiance demanded by Christ is both total and for life. Sometimes when there is a clash of loyalties a choice has to be made between Christ and another, between God's way and man's way, and for the Christian the choice is clear. To obey may mean to suffer for Christ's sake, which is a privilege (Matt. 10:34–7; Phil. 1:29). The Christian also has to fight daily a warfare against powerful temptation and sin (Phil. 1:27–8; Eph. 6:10–20).

The radical ethic makes demands within and without and brings into being a life-style which may incur suffering and ridicule; but it is the ethic of the Lord.

Following the Lord Jesus

In the days when Jesus lived in Galilee and Judea he called men to leave home and follow him, promising to make them 'fishers of men' (Mark 1:16–20). Levi, the tax collector, heard the call of Jesus and then 'got up, left everything, and followed him' (Luke 5:27–8). Over the centuries the motif of following Jesus has always been strong in the Church, even though it has had different expressions at different times and places.

Such a passage as Mark chapter 8 verses 34–8 has had, and continues to have, a tremendous impact upon not only Christians but also upon those who are considering the challenge of Christ addressed to them:

If anyone wants to come with me ... he must forget self, carry his cross, and follow me. For whoever wants to save his own life will lose it; but whoever loses his life for me and for the gospel will save it. Does a person gain anything if he wins the whole world but loses his life? Of course not! There is nothing he can give to regain his life. If a person is ashamed of me and of my teaching in this godless and wicked day, then the Son of Man will be ashamed of him when he comes in the glory of his Father with the holy angels.

One thinks of the *Imitation of Christ* by Thomas à Kempis (died 1471), the example of Francis of Assisi (died 1226) and the vows of chastity, poverty and obedience taken by monks and nuns as expressions of following Christ in Europe in the Middle Ages.

For many other Christians, then and since in a variety of traditions and denominations, the following of Jesus the Master has meant and still means at least two things. First of all it involves following the example of Jesus—his dedication to the will of the Father, his resisting of temptation, his humility, his love and concern for others, his prayer life and his desire that all should know and love God (1 Pet. 2:21). Secondly it means obeying the commandments that he gave to those who would be disciples of the kingdom of God. Some of these we considered above as part of the radical ethic.

Evangelical Protestant teaching has usually explained following Jesus as a disciple in terms of forsaking selfishness and sin in one's past life (as the disciples of old left their nets and families) and of confessing and obeying Christ in the whole of life (as the disciples physically followed Jesus everywhere and eventually confessed that he was Messiah).[1] For many people this way of understanding the demands of the Lord Christ has been instrumental, under God and by his grace, of producing true godliness and Christian commitment.

Others, who would not care to be called Evangelicals, have seen the Christian life in similar terms. Commenting on the theme of taking up the cross and following Jesus the late C. S. Lewis put the following words into the mouth of Jesus as he addresses a would-be disciple today.

> Give me all. I don't want so much of your time and so much of your money and so much of your work: I want you. I have not come to torment your natural self, but to kill it. No half-measures are any good. I don't want to cut off a branch here and a branch there, I want to have the whole tree down. I don't want to drill the tooth, or crown it, or stop it, but have it out. Hand over the natural self, all the desires which you think innocent as well as the ones you think wicked—the whole outfit. I will give you a new self instead. In fact I will give you myself; my own will shall become yours.[2]

Lewis then makes the point that the same Lord Jesus who makes such demands also says: 'The yoke I will give you is easy, and the load I will put on you is light' (Matt. 11:30). Only those who take up the cross know how the yoke is easy; it is part of the miracle of grace.

Walking and living in Christ

Another method of describing the Christian life, which draws its inspiration primarily from the Epistles of Paul and to a lesser extent from John's Gospel, is to speak of walking in or living in Christ. This means walking and living in the body of Christ, in vital union with the Head who is Christ the Lord. The basis for this way of talking is found for example in Colossians chapter 2 verses 6–7 where Paul wrote: 'Since you have accepted Christ Jesus as Lord, live in union with him. Keep your roots deep in him, build your lives on him, and become stronger in your faith, as you were taught.' The verb which is translated 'live in union' may also be translated 'walk in' him. Then there are the lovely words of Jesus recorded by John: 'I am the vine, and you are the branches. Whoever remains in me, and I in him, will bear much fruit; for you can do nothing without me' (John 15:5). Here the necessary union of the branch with the stem of the vine is used to illustrate the necessary union of Christians with their Head, who gives them eternal life.

Paul described the life of the pagan and non-Christian in terms of 'walking in' or 'living in' sin (Col. 3:7; Eph. 2:2). Another way of expressing the wordly life-style is to 'walk after the flesh' (Rom. 8:4 RV). The Good News Bible translates the latter expression as living 'according to human nature' which means following the natural desires of the heart and the mind, which without Christ's rule, are sinful. The manner in which people follow their natural desires is of course to some extent socially and culturally determined, although at the root of the different expressions are such powerful motivations as selfishness, greed, anger, envy, indecency and idolatry. This is another way of saying that sin is in essence the same when committed in different cultures by different races, castes and classes of human beings.

In contrast to walking in the standards of fallen human nature the Christian, as was stated earlier, lives and walks in Christ and in his standards. By faith he is eternally united to Christ in his body the Church and in his new race, the redeemed humanity, for whom God is preparing the new heavens and new earth. By the grace of God, the believer is justified through saving faith and is adopted into the family of God. Adoption is the greatest privilege under the gospel (1 John 3:1). It has been rightly said that:

> You sum up the whole of the New Testament teaching in a single phrase, if you speak of it as a revelation of the Fatherhood of the holy Creator. In the same way, you sum up the whole of New Testament religion if you describe it as the knowledge of one's holy Father. If you want to judge how well a person understands Christianity, find out how much he makes of the thought of being God's child, and having God as his Father. If this is not the thought that prompts and controls his worship and prayers and his whole outlook on life, it means that he does not understand Christianity very well at all. For everything that Christ taught ... everything that is distinctively Christian as opposed to Jewish, is summed up in the knowledge of the Fatherhood of God. 'Father' is the Christian name for God.[3]

To be in Christ is to have God as Father. And it is on the basis of being in Christ that Paul can describe the Christian life in such wonderful terms as sharing the resurrection life of Christ (Rom. 6), living in the power of the Spirit of Christ (Rom. 8) and being exalted into heaven with Christ (Eph. 1). To walk in and live in Christ is to remember daily and hourly that God loves us in Christ, that God is our Father, that Christ supplies us with every need and that we are to live in his power.

If being a Christian is to walk in the Lord Jesus it is also to 'walk in the Spirit'. Twice in the Epistle to the Galatians Paul uses the verb 'to walk' in terms of the relationship of the believer to the Spirit who indwells him and guides him. 'Walk by the Spirit and ye shall not fulfil the lusts of the flesh' (5:16 RV) and 'If we live by the Spirit, by the Spirit let us also walk' (5:25 RV). Between these two passages Paul lists the produce of human nature and the produce of the Spirit within man. From one comes immoral and indecent actions and words whereas from the other comes love, joy and peace. To walk in Christ is to be dominated by the indwelling Spirit who produces beautiful fruit in the life, fruit which God delights to see. Though Christianity is necessarily Christ-centred it is empowered by the Holy Spirit. The verb 'let us walk' (Gal. 5:25) literally means 'let us walk together as soldiers march in line'. This reminds us that walking in the Spirit is also a walking with others who are indwelt by the same Spirit.

Walking and living in Christ is also a 'walking in faith'. 'For our life is a matter of faith,' said Paul, 'not of sight' (2 Cor. 5:7). As yet we cannot see with our eyes the exalted Lord but we walk 'in him' towards him in the power of the Spirit. Trusting in him and his sure promises of grace we are strengthened and directed by him towards our heavenly home. This insight that the life of the Christian and the Christian community is a walking by faith was at the centre of the great Evangelical (Methodist) Revival of the eighteenth century and can still be appreciated in the hymns of Charles Wesley, William Cowper and John Newton.

Paul also described the Christian life in terms of walking in holiness (Eph. 2:10, 4:1–2), of walking in love (Eph. 5:2; Rom. 14:15) and of walking in the light (Eph. 5:8–13). John wrote in similar terms: 'My children, our love should not be just words and talk; it must be true love, which shows itself in action' (1 John 3:18). There is no contradiction involved in speaking of walking in Christ, in the Spirit, by faith and in love, for the Christian life is Christ centred, Spirit empowered, trusting in God and productive of good works which glorify the Father who is in heaven.

It is interesting to observe that the majority of the verbs translated 'to walk' by the Revised Version and which relate to our theme are in the plural. Now the obvious reason for this is that the people addressed were members of a community and thus the plural was the appropriate number of the verb. Yet the plural is a useful reminder to us that the Christian life can never be an individualistic experience (unless by God's providence an individual had to live on a desert island). I do not walk in Christ by the Spirit by faith on my own; I walk with others and the whole fellowship to which I belong is engaged in this walking together. We thus help each other; when one stumbles the others pick him up; when one is held back by problems others help him to sort them out. The whole community, the local body of Christ, is then walking towards the goal of perfection: 'Finally, brethren, we beseech and exhort you in the Lord Jesus, that, as ye received of us how ye ought to walk and to please God, even as ye do walk—that ye abound more and more' (1 Thess. 4:1 RV). Jesus called his disciples to be perfect as our Father is perfect; Paul called Christians to 'abound more and more' in holiness, love and good works.

Guidance

The confession that Jesus Christ is a personal Lord inevitably carries with it the expectation that the Christian will be guided in every part of his life by the Lord. The way in which this guidance is understood and received differs from one type of Christian to another as well as from one group to another. For example in some churches which are called 'charismatic' by outsiders and 'renewed' by those within them, there is often a strong belief that the leaders are there to guide and counsel, in Christ's name and power, members of the fellowship. Thus the guidance of Christ the Lord is understood as being mediated through the elders. To change a job, move house, adopt a child, court a boy or girl, buy a car, or take part in other activities, is only undertaken after the elders have given their permission. Since submission to those above you in the Lord is a strong theme in the New Testament (1 Pet. 5:5) there is much to be said for this view. The danger attached to it is that if it is done consistently over a period of time an individual Christian may begin to lose the exercise of the priority of conscience in his own life and may also begin to lose his sense of personal responsibility to God for his actions and words.

In the traditional Evangelical setting, guidance is often understood as occurring in a much more individualistic way. As the Christian faces making a decision, be it a large or small one, he fervently prays to the Lord to guide him. Then he may open his Bible hoping for some appropriate text to jump up from the page towards which his eyes look. Or, he may hope for an appropriate message in the brief exposition in the notes which he uses when reading the Bible. He may also begin to look for

God's answer to his prayer in the circumstances of the day. So he listens carefully to what everybody says to him, he looks hopefully at all the circumstances in which he finds himself, especially noting any peculiar ones which may be saying to him, 'this is the way for you to go'. Further, he may talk to a friend asking for his advice or he may see his pastor.

It is a sure fact that this individualistic approach to guidance is both time-consuming and energy-consuming, for the searching may go on for a long time and devour nervous strength needed for the ordinary demands of everyday life. It is regrettable that so many Christian students who are facing final examinations appear to spend so much time in this type of activity and thereby perhaps penalise themselves in terms of the standard of the degree they take.

What can we say in a few sentences about this real problem? Is there a via media between the total submission to elders and the totally individualistic approach? First, we can joyfully affirm that God is good and, though we may seek guidance in strange ways (for instance casting lots) he is gracious and so manages, in the end, to cause us to end up in the place where he wants us to be—that is presuming we were sincere in the prayer for the Lord to guide.

Secondly, we can say that Christ the Lord has a purpose for each of our lives and that he, more than we ourselves, desires that we perfectly fulfil that purpose.

Thirdly, we can be confident what he wants us to pray to God our Father, whose adopted children we are, in his name, making all our requests known to him.

Fourthly, we can be thankful that since Christ has given gifts to the churches to lead and to teach his people then he will use these gifts to lead us. So we are to make full use of the advice and guidance of pastors, teachers and leaders and we are to ask the brothers and sisters to pray for us as we pray that God will guide them as they guide us.

Fifthly, we are to remember that the major aspect of the will of God for our lives is that we should be holy (1 Thess. 4:3–4). Jesus said that the first concern should be to seek the kingdom of God our Father and to leave the rest to God (Matt. 6:33). This appears to tell us that as we seek to live and walk in Christ towards the perfection Jesus set before us guidance will find its proper level in our lives.

Finally, we can say that in our reading of the Bible we should not be looking for 'texts' on which to hang our future; rather we should be learning the whole contents of God's revelation so that its major themes, principles and demands are made a part of our mind and thinking processes; this embedded structure will then be in our minds as the word of the living God to set the context for receiving the advice of others and finally making a decision.

A PRAYER

O God of heaven and earth, how grateful I am that for the sake of Jesus Christ you call me your child. May I truly follow him and take up my cross as his disciple; may I always live in the knowledge that my walk is in him and that I have therefore died to sin, and may I ever know his leading in my life, for I pray in his name. Amen.

NOTES
[1] See for example, J. R. W. Stott, *Basic Christianity* (1958).
[2] C. S. Lewis, *Mere Christianity* (1974 ed.), pp. 163–4.
[3] J. I. Packer, *Knowing God* (1975 ed.), p. 224.

Appendix:
The Reformers and the Ascension

EARLIER WE QUOTED the relevant clauses from the Apostles' and Nicene Creeds on the ascension and session of Christ. At this point, having summarised the theology of the Ascension as given in the New Testament it is worth noting how the Protestant Reformers, in the demanding and exciting period of the middle of the sixteenth century, interpreted the ascension of Christ. The following extracts are from the Scottish Confession (1560), which in recent days has been studied afresh in Scotland, the Belgic Confession (1561), which was revised by the famous international Synod of Dort (1618), and the Heidelberg Catechism (1563)—perhaps the most famous of all Protestant catechisms.

The Scottish Confession

> We do not doubt but that the selfsame body which was born of the virgin, was crucified, dead, and buried, and which did rise again, did ascend into the heavens, for the accomplishment of all things, where in our name and for our comfort He has received all power in heaven and earth, where He sits at the right hand of the Father, having received His kingdom, the only advocate and mediator for us. Which glory, honour, and prerogative, He alone amongst the brethren shall possess till all His enemies are made His footstool, as we undoubtedly believe they shall be in the Last Judgment. We believe that the same Lord Jesus shall visibly

return for this Last Judgment as He was seen to ascend. And then, we firmly believe, the time of refreshing and restitution of all things shall come, so that those who from the beginning have suffered violence, injury, and wrong, for righteousness' sake, shall inherit that blessed immortality promised them from the beginning. But, on the other hand, the stubborn, disobedient, cruel persecutors, filthy persons, idolators, and all sorts of the unbelieving, shall be cast into the dungeon of utter darkness, where their worm shall not die, nor their fire be quenched. The remembrance of that day, and of the Judgment to be executed in it, is not only a bridle by which our carnal lusts are restrained but also such inestimable comfort that neither the threatening of worldly princes, nor the fear of present danger or of temporal death, may move us to renounce and forsake that blessed society which we, the members, have with our Head and only Mediator, Christ Jesus: whom we confess and avow to be the promised Messiah, the only Head of His Kirk, our just Lawgiver, our only High Priest, Advocate, and Mediator. To which honours and offices, if man or angel presume to intrude themselves, we utterly detest and abhor them, as blasphemous to our sovereign and supreme Governor, Christ Jesus.

(Chapter XI, The Ascension)

The Belgic Confession

We believe that we have no access unto God save alone through the only Mediator and Advocate, Jesus Christ the righteous, who therefore became man, having united in one person the divine and human natures, that we men might have access to the divine

Majesty, which access would otherwise be barred against us. But this Mediator, whom the Father hath appointed between him and us, ought in nowise to affright us by his majesty, or cause us to seek another according to our fancy. For there is no creature, either in heaven or on earth, who loveth us more than Jesus Christ; *who, though he was in the form of God, yet made himself of no reputation, and took upon him the form of a man and of a servant for us, and was made like unto his brethren in all things.* If, then, we should seek for another mediator, who would be well affected towards us, whom could we find who loved us more than he who laid down his life for us, even when we were his enemies? And if we seek for one who hath power and majesty, who is there that hath so much of both as *he who sits at the right hand of his Father*, and who hath *all power in heaven and on earth?* And who will sooner be heard than the own well-beloved Son of God?

Therefore it was only through diffidence that this practice of dishonoring instead of honoring the saints was introduced, doing that which they never have done nor required, but have, on the contrary, steadfastly rejected, according to their bounden duty, as appears by their writings. Neither must we plead here our unworthiness; for the meaning is not that we should offer our prayers to God on account of our own worthiness, but only on account of the excellence and worthiness of our Lord Jesus Christ, whose righteousness is become ours by faith.

Therefore the Apostle, to remove this foolish fear or, rather, distrust from us, justly saith that *Jesus Christ was made like unto his brethren in all things, that he might be a merciful and faithful high-priest, to make reconciliation for the sins of the people. For in that he himself hath suffered, being tempted, he is able to succor them that are tempted.* And further to encourage us, he adds: *Seeing, then, that we have a great high-priest that is passed into the heavens, Jesus the Son of God, let us hold fast our profession. For we have not a high-priest which can not be touched with the feeling of our infirmities; but was in all points tempted like as we are, yet without sin. Let us therefore come boldly unto the throne of grace, that we may obtain mercy, and find grace to help in time of need.* The same Apostle saith: *Having boldness to enter into the holiest by the blood of Jesus, let us draw near with a true heart in full assurance of faith,* etc. Likewise, *Christ hath an unchangeable priesthood, wherefore he is able also to save them to the uttermost that come unto God by him, seeing he ever liveth to make intercession for them.* What more can be required? since Christ himself saith: *I am the way, and the truth, and the life; no man cometh unto the Father but by me.* To what purpose should we then seek another advocate, since it hath pleased God to give us his own Son as our Advocate? Let us not forsake him to take another, or rather to seek after another, without even being able to find him; for God well knew, when he gave him to us, that we were sinners.

Therefore, according to the command of Christ, we call upon the heavenly Father through Jesus Christ, our only Mediator, as we are taught in the Lord's Prayer: being assured that whatever we ask of the Father in his name will be granted us.

(Article XXVI, Of Christ's Intercession)

Q. 46. *How do you understand the words: 'He ascended into heaven'?*

A. That Christ was taken up from the earth into heaven before the eyes of his disciples and remains there on our behalf until he comes again to judge the living and the dead.

Q. 47. *Then, is not Christ with us unto the end of the world, as he has promised us?*

A. Christ is true man and true God. As a man he is no longer on earth, but in his divinity, majesty, grace and Spirit, he is never absent from us.

Q. 48. *But are not the two natures in Christ separated from each other in this way, if the humanity is not wherever the divinity is?*

A. Not at all; for since divinity is incomprehensible and everywhere present, it must follow that the divinity is indeed beyond the bounds of the humanity which it has assumed, and is nonetheless ever in that humanity as well, and remains personally united to it.

Q. 49. *What benefit do we receive from Christ's ascension into heaven?*

A. First, that he is our Advocate in the presence of his Father in heaven. Second, that we have our flesh in heaven as a sure pledge that he, as the Head, will also take us, his members, up to himself. Third, that he sends us his Spirit as a counterpledge by whose power we seek what is above, where Christ is, sitting at the right hand of God, and not things that are on earth.

Q. 50. *Why is there added: 'And sits at the right hand of God'?*

A. Because Christ ascended into heaven so that he might manifest himself there as the Head of his Church, through whom the Father governs all things.

Q. 51. *What benefit do we receive from this glory of Christ, our Head?*

A. First, that through his Holy Spirit, he pours out heavenly gifts upon us, his members. Second, that by his power he defends and supports us against all our enemies.